MORE PRAISE FOR
PICTURE YOUR BUSINESS STRATEGY

"The traditional methods of strategic communication rarely achieve the result expected by the author. This book enables you to engage stakeholders in the development of business strategy that results in mutual understanding and unprecedented organizational change. Are you tired of ineffective corporate communication? If so, this book is for you."

—JESSE WHITE, President, Intact Technology

"Strategic planning is daunting. I couldn't believe how in a few fun hours we were able to get everything about our business up on a map, identify the priorities, and determine next steps. When we revisited the map later—we were astounded at how much we had actually accomplished in 18 months— we plotted our success and realized it. We will use this approach again and again—it really works!"

—KEN MORRISON AND MAURO HERNANDEZ, owners, K&M Wines

PICTURE YOUR BUSINESS STRATEGY

Transform Decisions with the Power of Visuals

Christine Chopyak

NEW YORK   CHICAGO   SAN FRANCISCO

LISBON   LONDON   MADRID   MEXICO CITY   MILAN

NEW DELHI   SAN JUAN   SEOUL   SINGAPORE

SYDNEY   TORONTO

1 2 3 4 5 6 7 8 9 0   DOC/DOC   1 9 8 7 6 5 4 3

ISBN 978-0-07-181502-4
MHID   0-07-181502-3

e-ISBN 978-0-07-181503-1
e-MHID   0-07-181503-1

Library of Congress Cataloging-in-Publication Data

Chopyak, Christine.
 Picture your business strategy : transform decisions with the power of visuals / by Christine Chopyak.
   pages cm
 Includes bibliographical references.
 ISBN 978-0-07-181502-4 (alk. paper) — ISBN 0-07-181502-3 (alk. paper)
 1. Strategic planning. 2. Decision making. 3. Visual analytics. I. Title.
 HD30.28.C535 2013
 658.4'012—dc23

                                                                    2013006958

McGraw-Hill Education books are available at special quantity discounts to use as premiums and sales promotions or for use in corporate training programs. To contact a representative, please visit the Contact Us pages at www.mhprofessional.com.

This book is printed on acid-free paper.

This book is dedicated to the
hidden artist that lies
waiting in every
businessperson.
Get out and draw!

The smartest ideas come from those who have learnt to surf
the unpredictable and the unexpected.

—John Hunt, *The Art of the Idea*

The only tool we have is to ride the wave of change. We can imagine it.
We can feel it. If you ride this wave, you can ride any wave.
The feeling you have with your body connects you to the world.

—Ulric Rudebeck

CONTENTS

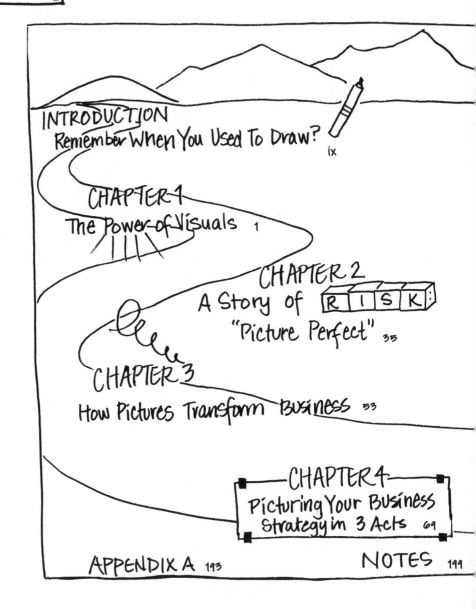

YOUR
BRIGHT FUTURE

INTRODUCTION

REMEMBER WHEN YOU USED TO DRAW?

I bet it wasn't that long ago that you happily grabbed a pencil, a crayon, a marker, or some other coloring medium and drew your ideas out onto the page. In the early days, the sun might have been purple, the grass yellow, and the mountains red, but you knew what they were, and you would draw them again and again, page after page. Do you remember the immense satisfaction you felt when you shared your picture with someone else, explaining what you had drawn as the person smiled and nodded in agreement?

When you were young, shapes were also fascinating. Parents or teachers would ask you to draw a "square," a "circle," or a "triangle." You would perfect these shapes the same way you perfected your handwriting or kicking a ball: you practiced them over and over again, in many colors, using overlapping images and sharing your shapes with teachers, parents, and friends.

As you got older, your artistic pursuits graduated from these simple drawings to coloring books (can you hear the teacher saying, "Stay within the lines"?) and then to other forms of copying and tracing—comic books; attempting to draw from "real life"; perhaps even "still lifes" and graffiti. Your drawings were not half bad, and the covers and insides of your notebooks were littered with images, doodles, and stuff you drew as you listened to the teachers go on and on about things that were old, irrelevant, and unimportant. In those days, it felt as if everyone was drawing something. Boys or girls—it really didn't matter. Like our music, our book covers and our notes to one another were an expression of ourselves, and they were art.

As you got older, you wrote fewer and fewer notes to your friends, and your notebook covers remained plain, with no color or images at all. Color became more important in what you wore and how you wore it than in a hand-drawn expression of something that you had seen or imagined. For those lucky few who got to go to art classes or who went on to be art majors in college, it was almost like an exclusive club. They were part of the "chosen." These were the people who had "talent" and were "creative." The rest of us (you and me) looked on longingly and with a little envy. What happened to the days when everyone got to do those things? Deep down inside, didn't a part of you want to go back to the days when you got to play with colors, paints, a canvas, some clay, or a camera and photos too?

It seems unfair that "artists" were separated from the rest of us. Haven't you always thought of yourself as at least a little creative? You may not be able to draw per se, but you do have a knack for solving puzzles, taking a photograph, arranging flowers, throwing a softball, or telling a story or a good joke. There is still a part of you that is in touch with that budding artist inside you. You create ways and opportunities for it to come out.

But, when we are faced with the prospect of drawing, the majority of us (adults) say immediately, "Are you crazy? I can't draw." I have heard this consistently from adults over the past 15 years. People stare at a blank piece of paper in a notebook or on the wall, and they panic. Their palms begin to sweat, and they look at others, saying out loud, "I really can't draw. I don't know what I am doing here." The big "rule book" in the universe says somewhere, "You didn't go to art school or do well in art class; therefore, you can't draw."

Your experience is my experience. There is nothing exceptional about my drawing. My parents tell me that I drew and doodled as a young adult to get extra credit in school. My homework and notebooks were very organized, illustrated, and colored. I got rid of coloring and pictures in my life as I worked as a beauty shop cleaner, a file clerk in a law firm, a fast-food cook, a regular line cook at low-end and high-end restaurants, and eventually a pastry chef. I edited medical journals and followed a calling to teach young people science in the shadow of the Shenandoah Mountains and the peaks of the Rocky Mountains in Keystone, Colorado.

I found business strategy before I rediscovered drawing and pictures. As the executive director at Keystone Science School in the mid-1990s, I was taught about business strategy by some of the country's brightest and most daring business leaders from DuPont, MeadWestvaco, and Amoco. Leaders from Nike, GM, and World Resources Institute schooled me in sustainable development and corporate social responsibility. Leaders from Ford Motor Company, the National Academy of Sciences, and the Pew Charitable Trusts challenged me to think about innovation in business, in education, and in systems. I experienced firsthand what happens when you link innovative thinking with sound business strategy through programs at North Carolina's Kenan-Flagler Business School and at Daniels College of Business at the University of Denver. It was through these interesting, mind-blowing, and challenging conversations and experiences that I discovered my natural inclination and deep passion for *strategy*.

I had significant "on-the-job" training through leading and learning. I participated in workshops and conferences run by business's best—Tom Peters, Peter Senge, and Stephen Covey—and I applied their models, experimented with them, failed, learned, and applied these models more thoughtfully and constructively. Realizing that I needed more formal business training, I enrolled in the Executive MBA Program at the Daniels College of Business, University of Denver, to get my business "mojo." At the same time, I met two of the cofounders at Alchemy: The Art of Transforming Business, who were strategic illustrators and business innovators: Janine Underhill and Patti Dobrowolski. While the MBA provided my B-school education, Janine and Patti mentored, coached, and supported my visual education. My love of strategy led me to consider combining processes and models with pictures. I rediscovered and experimented with images, words, color, and metaphor by drawing my way through a traditional MBA program. My visual "faculty" members never once told me that I couldn't draw. Patti and Janine helped me think and translate what I was learning into pictures. They asked me why I chose the images I did, how I thought, and how I organized images on a page. They taught me how to incorporate deep listening into my work so that I could

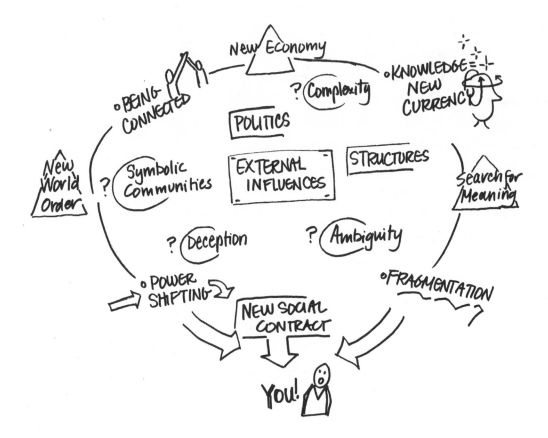

capture more information faster and more accurately. After a lot of practice and risk taking, I began to believe that I *could* draw. My colleagues in my MBA class made fun of my drawing, but at the same time they were intrigued by what I was doing. How could I get all the notes from a two- or three-hour lecture on one page? In spite of their ribbing, they frequently asked for copies of my "notes."

I began to take my learning outside my notebooks and work with people, cultures, and their systems. I began to see how pictures could help clarify complexities, simplify key concepts and messages, and inspire people to act. I learned early on that people always knew what I was drawing regardless of how "good" the drawing was. My simple, easy-to-draw images created the context that allowed the business strategy that people created to come alive. Even though I still had doubts about the quality of my drawings—were they ever "good enough"?—the teams I worked with understood the images and took their new pictures as the business equivalent of a "game plan."

The connection between pictures and strategy really clicked into place for me when I moved to London with my husband. Divided by a common language, the English, Scots, Welsh, and Irish helped me "see" different parts of the English language. When portrayed visually, the cultural richness of these four different regions stood out. The business pictures said more about how these people worked, what mattered to them, and their diverse sense of humor than any book or paper could. From a base in London, I had the privilege of meeting, working for, and creating with people from all over the world. These relationships, businesses, and colleagues continue to inform and influence my thinking about pictures and strategy in new ways every day.

Throughout 2012, *Fast Company* magazine wrote about Generation Flux. This is a tribe I fit in with, a group of businesspeople

I belong to. Like you, I have "fluxed" and "flubbed." I have taken risks and succeeded, taken other risks and not been so lucky. I have learned how to be a good leader, how to turn organizations around financially, and how to let go of smart, good people. I have also been able to find other such people in an intensely competitive landscape. I have been through more changes than I care to remember, and I continue to be lucky enough to create programs and products and watch them take off.

The one constant throughout all my "fluxing" has been my sketchpad and pen. I have gotten through good times and bad times by drawing pictures that I never thought I could draw. I was synthesizing, simplifying, and clarifying the world I lived and worked in with pictures, colors, and words.

Grab a journal and a pen. Use the shapes you know and love—circles, squares, triangles, and arrows. Draw a picture and see your world. You will find more possibilities than you can imagine!

CHAPTER 1

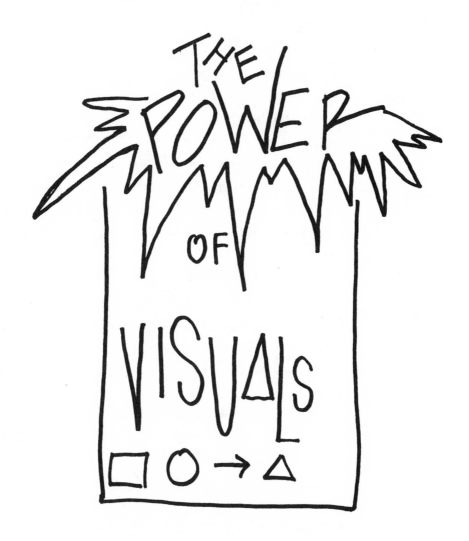

THE POWER OF VISUALS

The sun was coming up over the dusty and hazy skyline of southeastern Beijing when our taxi made a U-turn and came to a stop in front of a large, industrial-looking building. "Is this it?" my fellow traveler, Susan, asked me. "Yeah, according to the map," I replied. The cabdriver hit his hand against the back of the seat to get our attention and pointed to the meter. Oh, yeah, he wanted to be paid, I thought. I dug into my bag, pulled out a handful of yuan, and handed them to him. We left the cab, guidebook in hand, and stood alone somewhere in Beijing on a Saturday morning.

We were in search of a famous antiques flea market that was held in some obscure corner of Beijing on Saturdays, and the map told us that we were close. We were in China for 10 days in 2001, a few short days before the world—business and every-thing in it—changed on 9/11. We had a short window in which to see Panjiayuan flea market and head back to the hotel to fly on to Xian. Panjiayuan is well known for its size, authentic items, and shrewd negotiating and as an off-the-beaten-path experience for the intrepid traveler. I was pretty sure that no one would speak English.

Regardless of how wonderful the market might be, we had to find it first. We were close, according to the map, but with all the street names in Chinese characters and the industrial look and feel of the area, we were caught off guard. There were no signs indicat-ing where we needed to be. We headed toward a building that had its lights on and was open, and had a look around—antiques. We looked at each other and the guidebook—Panjiayuan was supposed to be outside.

We went to the counter and asked if anyone could speak English; they smiled and shook their heads no. I got out the map and pointed to the place where the flea market "should be"; they smiled, got excited, and started pointing and talking. They were giving us directions, but we could not understand them! I got out a pen, pointed to the map and the location, handed the pen to them, and nodded, my eyebrows raised: draw it! "Show me!"

A woman with kind eyes took the pen and drew a series of arrows: around the building, down a narrow street, right, then left, and then we would be there. She proudly handed the map back to me. "Xiè, xiě" (thank you, thank you), we smiled, repeated, and headed for the door.

After a few twists and turns, we arrived at a *huge* parking lot, partially draped with long, faded pieces of orange and red fabric to protect merchandise from the sun. Some items were on tables; others were delicately placed on the ground on top of sturdy rugs. The place was buzzing with people setting up and viewing the items that were on display. Almost everyone there had a sturdy, decorative steel thermos from which steaming green tea was poured and shared. There were large pieces of furniture along the edges of the market: wardrobes and intricately decorated chairs that looked as though they were made for royalty, of dark wood with brass fixtures.

Despite the early hour, people were doing a brisk business. Shoppers would point to items and ask how much. I observed them beginning the obligatory bartering negotiation that is part of any Chinese purchase unless you are at Walmart China. We walked the aisles, admiring handcrafted textiles, wooden carvings, brass and crystal glasses, hand-painted porcelain vases, statues of cranes, and classic Chinese drawings with calligraphy, waterfalls, and lovely, demure women.

"What are you looking for?" Susan asked. "What aren't we looking for? The stuff here is amazing—it's beautiful and intricate, even if it isn't 'old,'" I replied. We were beside a section that had a variety of birdcages of all sizes. Some were simple, made of plain pine wood and deep red cherry wood, and all were intricately carved. Beside the birdcages sat a series of locks with combinations, keys, or a series of twists to open them. Most were made of brass, but a few were made of wood and some of ivory.

We browsed the aisles with the Chinese salespeople looking at us strangely with big smiles. After a couple of hours, we had to head back. I refused to leave empty-handed. I kept coming back to those neat brass locks I had seen earlier. Where were they? As the parking lot was massive, finding that stall would probably take another hour or so.

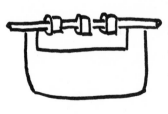

I tried to find someone who spoke English—no luck. I wandered up and down trying to retrace my steps, but time was running out. Finally I reached into my bag, took out a pen and a piece of scrap paper, and drew a picture of a lock on the back.

It was a crude drawing, but nonetheless, the vendor watching me started talking rapidly, pointing to an isolated corner of the market. He grabbed my paper and my pen and drew a birdcage. I smiled—we had connected! He showed me to the stall, showed the owner my drawing, and we all laughed. I made my purchase, negotiating all the while, and left the market.

This story is not unique; many of us have traveled to places where we don't speak the language. We use sign language, gestures, pantomime, and other visual ways to convey emotion, communicate, get what we need, or find help. Ironically, we have been doing this for centuries. The human ability to communicate creatively and understand one another began not with language but with pictures. The artifacts that we see today left on the inside of caves throughout the world are special stories that were passed down to younger generations. Daily stories were probably drawn in the sand with a stick or a rock. In his article "Better Learning and Expressing of Learning Through Visual Literacy," Professor Harry G. Tuttle from Syracuse University shares, "Our cave ancestors were visually literate; their lives depended on how well they could visually read the world around them."

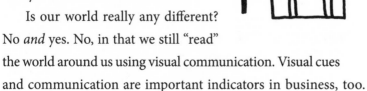

Is our world really any different? No *and* yes. No, in that we still "read" the world around us using visual communication. Visual cues and communication are important indicators in business, too.

There are signs that people are in agreement: customers desire a product, and employees have bought into a concept and a strategy.

Yes, the world is different in the twenty-first century. Access to technology, the rise of more affluent populations across the planet, and globalization have profoundly affected the way we see, read, and deal with the world around us. The number of people who travel and work virtually in multiple geographies and cultures every day has risen at a meteoric rate. The world demands language agility and cultural awareness, given the globalization of the marketplace.

In spite of the best that the technical world can offer, we have *not* found innovative ways to communicate or eliminate language barriers. However, visual images and pictures help people talk through and agree on strategy and product design. They also help individuals and teams think about, explore, and articulate how to achieve success and what it takes to execute their strategy. While English may be a default language in a global marketplace, pictures can be universally embraced and used by people from the factory floor to the boardroom. Pictures can raise issues that are culturally sensitive, subtle, or controversial. They provide a backdrop and a landscape for addressing barriers to organizational success. At the end of the business day, business quarter, or fiscal year, teams and their leaders can use pictures to have meaningful and relevant conversations about risk, reward, targets, and success.

This book makes an argument for the deliberate use of simple, hand-drawn pictures and images when we develop business strategy in order to transform how we make decisions, how we work together, and how we ultimately achieve results. So, how can better use of visuals help us do this?

Like the map and the travel guide I used to find my way to the antiques flea market, a picture of where the business is going is extremely useful. A city or street map allows us to see where we are and where we want to go. There are usually several ways to get to your destination, and a map can help you select either the most direct or the most scenic route. The same is true when you create a picture of your business strategy.

A picture contains your ideas, describes the tools you will use, and indicates who will do the job. Much like a map that has landmarks, crossroads, and highways, your visual business strategy can help the members of a team see the condition of the business based on the information that they share and what gets drawn. As the team shares information about financial, product, and customer success, rough and even crude stick-figure-type images and metaphors are used to picture these things. As the team members talk about what they want the business to accomplish and how they think they can get there, the whole strategy is pictured, not just a portion of it. By viewing the whole picture, teams can make choices about which direction to take and why—just like choosing the scenic route or the highway on a car trip across a country. Pictures help illuminate what choices you have and help the team determine the best route to take to achieve the desired outcome and results. Because a picture engages the imagination, multiple business scenarios can be created and evaluated quickly and easily with the use of pictures. Different routes produce different results. Together, the team members can assess and evaluate, "If we do this, then what will happen?" The team and the business can pick from a set of pictures that provide the best strategy and images of the path forward to deliver value.

Another way in which pictures can help us achieve great business results is through clarifying issues and identifying the things that are blocking our success. With the advent of GPS and satellite navigation systems, we can plan a route, pinpoint where we are in relation to that route, and identify whether there is roadwork or a traffic jam that will impede our ability to get to our final destination. With the aid of this visual guide, we can choose another way that will let us avoid the obstacles. We feel more in control of our choices because we can see them.

Pictures of a business process or strategy allow us to see many aspects of the business on one page. They show us the "whole picture" and pinpoint where we are in that picture. These images will also pinpoint where we are in enough detail so that we can see where we took a "wrong turn" or that we have been in a "traffic jam" without even knowing it. Pinpointing issues in a complex multinational business is a challenge. There are so many variables to consider— different regions of the world, different production schedules, different cultures, different people, and myriad ways of reporting. Pictures move above the granular and show the essence, the context, and the relevant content of the business. These pictures are not a list of the good, the bad, or the ugly. Rather, they are a synthesis of a system, with all its parts, pieces, and relationships. This kind of visual synthesis shows the connections among the different pieces in the system, making it much easier for teams to look at a visual and pinpoint success factors, areas of concern, and barriers that are in the way of progress and success.

Pictures are also a catalyst for team engagement and commitment. Think about what happens when you return from a vacation and you share your pictures with other people online through a file-sharing service or on Facebook. People ask questions about where you went, how long you stayed, and where you stayed. They comment on places they have visited or always wanted to. They want to know "How hard was it to get around?" and "What did you eat?" The viewers see the people you met and those you traveled with. Stories of the trip emerge as different images trigger different memories. Viewers get involved in your pictures of the trip almost as if they were there themselves. They put themselves in your shoes and see what you saw; they share what you experienced. These photos inspire and engage the viewers—they are a break from the "real world."

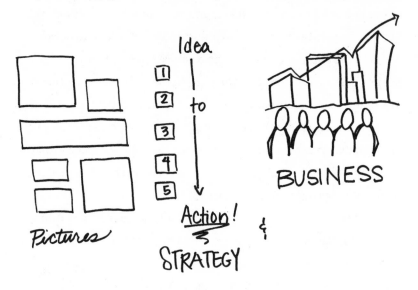

Consider what could happen if you shared a picture of a business strategy with the members of your team or with everyone in your company in the same way that you share photos of your travels. People like this form of visual/story engagement, particularly if they were there when the "pictures" were created. A visual business strategy that was designed and built by everyone on the team is exciting. The pictures, colors, and metaphors work the same way travel photos work—the team members recall what they discussed, how the work they do needs to change, and what actions are needed along the way. They point out places where people "signed up" for different parts of the plan. They can tell who is accountable for what and what commitments were made. They also share what got them excited and "what's next" for them. The picture of the business strategy engages, motivates, and aligns people on a team and in a business when they have helped create the visual that shows where they are going, what the outcomes will be, and how to get there.

Ultimately, picturing your business strategy can streamline communication. We can simplify and clarify key actions and activities while creating new efficiencies. With the right information and team participation, the pictures reveal opportunities and transform the quality and the results of your decisions. Making this a reality is not as difficult as you might think. We need to tap into our ability to think in pictures. We had that ability and confidence in it when we were children. As we got older, we swapped our visual language for characters that form our oral and written traditions.

BACKGROUND: PICTURES, STRATEGY, AND BUSINESS

In the Beginning, There Were Pictures . . .

Young children think and cognitively process in pictures before they speak because language, in the brain, is a higher cognitive function. The full set of senses plays a complete role in a child's abilities to process and "read" the world around him. With heightened senses, smells, tastes, colors, and sounds become associated with shapes and colors. We connect these images to the sensory input and eventually, with repetition over time, children and adults connect them to words.

Think about the picture books that you had as a child or that you use with your children. They exist for a reason—to connect images, textures, feelings, colors, and shapes to words. Picture books like this for young children are global in their application. Walk into any bookstore or library in any city in any country and you will find these simple picture books. They are colorful, with simple images, and they connect these images to language and to culture. Images (icons) that are connected to words through repetition become familiar to a child. As the brain continues to develop our language abilities, which are found in what is called Broca's area, we continue to connect images to words, and eventually to sentences and whole paragraphs, and language is born.

As we mature, written and oral language take over, and the "picture books" of our youth give way to dense 200- to 800-page texts, most of them devoid of images or pictures. Ironically, "Today our students are visually literate within their world of 'electronic images' such as TV, videogames, and the Web; they want to be visually literate in their school which is often devoid of visuals," Professor Harry Tuttle laments. Our desire to continue to use images along with words has contributed to the rise in popularity of graphic novels. While images and icons help us "read" the adult world, pictures, as one of the learning styles—visual, kinesthetic, and auditory—get sidelined in favor of written texts or lecture-style delivery in classrooms, office meetings, and boardrooms. Words dominate our lives, while pictures provide supplemental and background information.

And yet, according to the U.S. Department of Labor, Occupational Safety & Health Administration (OSHA), "educational researchers suggest that approximately 83% of human learning occurs visually, and the remaining 17% through the other senses—11% through hearing, 3.5% through smell, 1% through taste, and 1.5% through touch." The study goes on to "suggest that three days after an event, people retain 10% of what they heard from an oral presentation, 35% from a visual presentation, and 65% from a (combined) visual and oral presentation." The majority of the population learns using pictures and images. Why don't we operate in more visual ways inside the businesses where we work? Why don't we use pictures to close the gap between employee engagement and business performance? Can we use pictures to do that?

Where Have All the Images Gone?

Good question. We are bombarded by marketing and media messages and visuals every day, so it is not as if we are devoid of any kind of visual communication (thankfully). These visuals are delivered to us in HD or high resolution, at angles, blurred, and in Technicolor. We consume these images, and our brain takes them all in, processes the interesting bits, determines some meaning, discards most of the material, and holds on to the things that are pleasing and relevant to us personally. For most marketing departments and agencies, repeating these visual messages is the standard—the more we see and hear a message, the more we will want the product or service. This is the external/consumer and commercial use of pictures. It seems that the "consumer" approach to using visuals as a means of selling something might make the same sense when used inside organizations. We could use pictures to sell, explain, and outline strategy.

One area where we see pictures in business is in the explanation of business models. Organizations use business models to explain certain financial, organizational, or structural aspects of business. Since the advent of the Industrial Revolution, academics and business professionals have created these models as a way to interpret, understand, and predict how businesses will perform under certain conditions. The field of strategy has many well-developed methods and models that can assist teams and leaders with all stages of strategy development. While the models are most often detailed in text to explain how they should be used, why, and what result an analysis might produce, simple, easy-to-understand pictures can also show the reader how the models work. And, they do it in one simple image. In *The Decision Book* by Mikael Krogerus, Roman Tschäppeler, Philip Earnhart, and Jenny Piening, 50 models for strategic thinking are summarized and visually portrayed. Each of the 50 models has a picture that accompanies the text and provides a quick overview of how the model works. Here are a couple of examples:

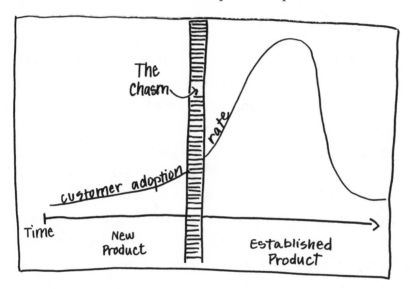

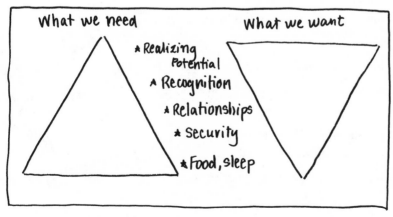

From The Decision Book: 50 Models for Strategic Thinking by Mikael Krogerus and Roman Tschäppeler, translated by Jenny Piening. Copyright © 2008 by Kein & Aber AG Zurich. English translation copyright © 2011 by Jenny Piening. Used by permission of W. W. Norton & Company, Inc.

Yes, there are words. But the words serve to *anchor* relevant content and context that facilitates the use of the visual model. If we are vaguely familiar with the models, the visual helps us remember the steps, the format, and the outcome. It's the combination of verbal cues combined with an image that helps our brain discern the right model, process, and image for the business challenge that we are trying to understand or solve. The combination of images and words is key to picturing your business strategy, as we will explore throughout this book. Let's first understand how these strategy models (in particular) can be used without pictures.

Business leaders and faculty of MBA programs would argue that the models are *theories*—ways to think about your business to ensure that you are considering all angles of market competition, from product opportunities to threats to profitability and strengths of performance. When companies use these models, the results typically end up in a presentation format—a long written list, with all the background and data printed and put into a giant binder, along with a slide deck for presenting the summary/ findings. The person, team, or consultants within the company who conducted the analysis present their interpretation of the results to management orally, with little assistance from pictures or images. As a business leader, when I received these kinds of analyses, I rarely saw the visual model applied, even though many of these models were drawn initially to show how they could be used and what kind of data one might expect from the results.

Furthermore, once the results have been presented, it is unusual to have them distributed across the company for general employee reaction, discussion, and problem solving. The perspective or insights of senior management are also left out. These presentations might be placed on the internal intranet for employees to read and review, but there are few times when a team or a division sits down as a whole unit and discusses what can be gleaned from such an analysis. People within the organization are not always consulted on their views or thoughts when the actual business model is applied. They may not be familiar with the business model, so when they see the results, they may think, "Who created *that*? That's not my experience. What does this have to do with what I do every day?"

Since we don't see the results or discuss them with our peers or colleagues, the ideas that are pertinent to our work get boiled down into something generic that doesn't apply to anyone in particular, and nothing sticks with us. Employees consume the message and discard it as quickly as it came in because there is little that resonates with them. The message itself is one-dimensional. There is nothing, emotionally or visually, to anchor the results or the recommendations needed into the brain. We learned earlier how much we retain when an oral presentation is made: three days after the presentation, we retain 10 percent. What happens one week after a presentation? How can we expect words to convey the urgency of making a business change? We want and need our employees to pay attention, and yet we deliver messages over and over that do not mean anything to employees specifically. This is not because the message is not important or relevant. It's because of how the message is presented. People are probably listening, but no one is remembering what is being said.

Strategy models are applied to develop a plan for the business going forward. These models can help us select the right route to accomplish a change, upgrade an approach, or better understand an opportunity. What might happen if, instead of the mammoth binder with pages of words in it, one or two simple images were combined with some key words that got my attention, as an employee? What if the images were linked to a whole set of other im-

ages that were specifically designed to engage me as an employee and provide me with a sense of urgency as well as direction? Would things change? There are some other "business habits" that we in business have developed that stand between us and our visual strategy. Let's clarify what these are so that we can recognize, know, and understand them. Once we understand what gets in our way, we are better positioned with a twenty-first-century sensibility to build a plan that includes other people, is memorable, makes it easy to see what and where the business is going, and provides greater assurance that the plan will happen and deliver results.

Bad Business Habits or Problem-Solving Traps

Have you ever noticed that we can spend minutes, hours, days, or lifetimes dissecting and mulling over why something failed and why it did not work? We are looking for the "root cause" of the problem. (Think about all the analysis that's done after elections, or when a major national disaster occurs.) *Root cause analysis*, a popular business strategy method, supports the notion that if we can get to the bottom of a problem, the solution will somehow be revealed to us. If we dig deep enough, we (the diggers who are trying to find the root) will find the answer that will "fix" the business problem. We have been educated into the idea that we can determine the solution only when we understand the problem completely.

In the industrial and technological ages, root cause analysis worked, and in some cases it still does. It is a linear, methodical, and mechanical approach to identifying solutions by deconstructing all aspects of the problem to identify the weak link and fix it. Six Sigma and other efficiency measurement tools have done a great deal to improve effectiveness in manufacturing, natural resource exploration, and product delivery using this approach. The solutions are tidy, well organized, and contained within the department in which the problem occurs. The process feels and is productive in identifying the aberration and correcting it once it has been isolated.

Unfortunately, what has worked in the past may not always work in the present or in the future. The fact is, this approach has diminishing returns in this emerging and ever-changing environment. In *That Used to Be Us*, the authors, Thomas L. Friedman and Michael Mandlebaum, interview Curtis Carlson, CEO of SRI International. SRI International is an "innovation factory" for everything "from education to clean energy to homeland security." Carlson explains, "There are few problems left today where one person with one skill can solve them. . . . More and more, innovation that happens from the top down tends to be orderly but dumb. Innovation that happens from the bottom up tends to be chaotic but smart."

Root cause analysis is primarily focused on a single "root"— the one or two things that can be modified or upgraded to make a meaningful and value-added change. However, the root may actually be "root*s*," with many issues affecting a larger problem. And, the roots may lie at different levels of the system and connect to other roots. As with a giant piece of string that connects the system, when you pull on one end, the other connecting points are also affected. How can we see and understand the dynamics of this many-layered system? Today, the one-person, one-root approach simply will not provide what's needed to solve a problem effectively. The complexity and dimensions of the problems and opportunities that we face today require different ways to see all the aspects that are involved.

Second, research from the field of Appreciative Inquiry at Case Western University has found that the farther you dig to solve the problem and the deeper the hole gets, the more information you uncover, with the result that the problem becomes less clear, more complicated, and downright confusing. Instead of providing us clarity and direction, too much information pushes us to dig deeper because we believe that more data will reveal the solution. Remember, in root cause analysis, we are in search of the *one* answer. In our attempt to get to the one root, we deconstruct every angle to understand what caused the difference between what we expected and what actually happened. Our desire is genuine and understandable. It is also misguided. The volumes of data that we unearth make it even more difficult to see what information is relevant and what can be discarded. Our fear is that we may discard something invaluable that holds the key to our solution, so we hold on to everything. We are paralyzed by our analysis, creating a feeling of being stuck, trapped, and unable to move.

THE REPTILIAN-BRAIN TRAP

As we get pressure from our bosses or others to solve a problem or come up with a solution, we feel that pressure bearing down on us, loaded with both expectation and the fear of failure. Our mood, attitude, and willingness sour as we focus on finding the one or "right" answer to the problem. As we get more concerned about the consequences of failure, our field of options and what we are willing to consider narrow—significantly. In this state, we get a slightly panicked feeling, succumbing to the part of the brain that controls our most basic instincts involving fear—should I flee, fight, or freeze? In this condition, we are less likely to ask questions, to be optimistic, or to be curious. We are seen as short-tempered, frustrated, and impatient.

The base of the brain, commonly referred to as the *brain stem*, has significant influence on our physical, emotional, and psychological behaviors and is called the basal ganglia or "reptilian brain." This is the part of the brain that in early humans helped us survive, signaling when we should run, freeze, or fight. While the environmental conditions that produce these stresses have changed from tigers to chronic professional concerns, our reptile brain has not changed in how it reacts to the stress. It signals to our endocrine system to pump up the adrenaline and get ready to address the challenge we face now with fear in tow.

Fear is a powerful and destabilizing emotion, to say the least. In the distant past, human encounters with their own fear were frequent, but short-lived. Either you survived to live another day or you didn't. In the twenty-first-century workplace, it is not uncommon for people to live with the pressure and a heightened state of anxiety for days, weeks, or even months or years. Data are clear about the emotional and physical consequences of this kind of perpetual state of being. We cannot sustain it for any long period of time, and it takes its toll on the individual, the team, and even the company.

The reptilian-brain trap prevents us from seeing the problem for what it really is (simple or complex, it doesn't matter). Our brains organize information and data in a way that is familiar to us to help us alleviate our panic, our fear. This pattern of behavior prevents us from connecting new information to old information or seeing new patterns that may lead toward some type of solution or resolution. Fear is contagious—it works in teams the same way it works in the individual. With time marching on, there is never enough time to get the job done, driving fear up and letting desperation set in.

THE "LOOKING OUTSIDE FOR HELP" TRAP

With the energy of the team waning, fatigue sets in. Some people have described this as feeling disoriented and confused. True desperation can take hold, and the team may feel that someone from

MANAGEMENT
CONSULTANT

the outside will be able to present things in a new light, thus revealing things that had previously been unseen. That outside person may even have the ability to identify the problem when the team members cannot because the team members are too close to it. Outsiders can often "see" things that we cannot or will not see.

Outsiders can also bring a rush of fresh energy into a problem-solving situation. When they arrive, armed with their analytics, models, and processes, business and management consultants may actually seem to us more like superheroes or sages. They are smart people ("Maybe they know something I don't know"), they are external ("Maybe they can see things I can't"), and they cost money ("I know they will find the answer!"). They become a light in the darkness of our search for the alternatives and answers. They are gurus of sorts.

As a business and management consultant myself, I run the risk of losing the respect of those I admire most, but someone has to say it: *the idea that a person from outside the organization can come into a business that she knows in a peripheral or even superficial way and, in a relatively short period of time, "solve the problem" or "create a solution" is crazy,* and *we know it is crazy.*

It is true that we as an organization can benefit from the expertise and perspective of these external professionals. They typically affirm that our problem is complex; sometimes they even ask for more or different data. They recommend some solutions and ask questions that are new to the group. They inject some new thinking and energy into the process. External consultants also buy us a little more time, and they assuage our deepest fears of not being smart enough or good enough at our jobs. With our consultant's report in hand, we pay the invoice and pore over the words in the document to find something we have not thought of or tried before. In the end, we are left as before: on our own with our team to find the solution and solve the problem. This trap, while eliciting new and different information and buying time, is costly, requires another layer of oversight of management time, and can often disenfranchise members of the team who wonder why external people were brought in. The pressure to find the solution to a problem is still facing the team, and we need to search for yet another way to solve the problem.

THE TECHNOLOGY TRAP

With a big report in hand and little in the way of answers, leaders and their teams are desperate to find a solution, or at least a pathway that will get them somewhere. Employees still want to be part of the solution, not the problem, so the team members go back to the analysis, the data, and other business tools designed to help identify problems and inspire solutions. The team psychs itself up to push the boundaries, consider new ways to look at the problem, and work harder.

But the team members have other responsibilities at work, and the demands on everyone's time are tight. Who has the time to incorporate yet another new thing into an overcrowded, fast-paced work environment? The team members are frustrated, and their morale is low. People who, at the beginning of the process, had some ideas about how to fix the problem are feeling marginalized. People who like to complete a task and tick the box are confounded. Pressure from senior leadership for "answers" is still there, money has been thrown at finding a solution, there are meetings taking place behind closed doors, and everyone is on edge.

As the team leader, we observe and feel this around us. We feel helpless and alone. We have tried, but we have failed, and we pull back. The same thing happens with the team members. They sense the futility and exasperation, and they pull away from one another. We stop talking and engaging with our colleagues. We feel as if everyone wants us to have the answers. Everyone feels the weight of responsibility for the collective performance. We hope we can come up with something, both because we cannot bear to let one another down and, to be honest, because we all just want to get on with our work, holding onto our job and our role in the company.

In a last-ditch effort, we turn to technology for an answer. This makes perfect sense to our business brains. In business, technological solutions for complex and persistent problems have been found in the past. Stories about technology saving the day have become part of how we think about solving a problem: "It's better, faster, cheaper." Technology is also accessible in the business environment. We use it to communicate, stay informed, create products, and talk to the world about what we do. In light of the universal access and interface, we hope this can help us produce solutions and provide clarity to the problem in ways that we have not seen before.

The new and emerging ways of working and communicating (texting, smartphones, Skype, videoconferencing, e-mail, Facebook, Ning, SharePoint, GoToMeeting, and so on) are great tools and great distractions. In *The Five Faces of Genius*, Annette Moser-Wellman refers to e-mail and other such distractions as the "administrative opiate." She goes on to challenge our thinking about the technology trap: "In order for imagination to lead implementation, we need to deprive ourselves of technology. . . . Use your head, not your keyboard" to communicate. "We waste more time trying to jam our thoughts into the parameters of the software than it would take to word process what we compose by hand. Don't let the computer dominate your creative process."

In spite of this, technology enablers dominate business life. We are more connected and plugged into work and one another than ever before. These enablers make it harder for people to be effective, productive, and energized. When the work environment is confusing and tensions are high, our technology devices provide the ideal escape and distraction. We retreat into our social and virtual networks, surf the Internet, talk online, and play games with people from all over the world. We isolate ourselves from our colleagues and from the problem, putting more distance between us and a possible solution.

The reality is that as a team, we are lost. We don't necessarily agree on the root of the problem, and we cannot individually or collectively see the solution. Given our common fatigue, frustration, and lack of connection, we turn to the things that help us *feel* more connected and a part of something. Instead of working on the problem together, we just want to make it all go away. We communicate virtually with our peers because we cannot look them in the face with the problem still looming. We are stuck. We know it, and they know it, but neither of us wants to admit it.

We have all experienced these problem-solving traps and bad business habits. While the conditions or circumstances may not have been exactly as I have described them, we know what it feels like to be stuck, locked in, and unable to move up and out of a situation. We are hesitant to follow the advice that is given by others.

Many teams and their leaders walk away at this point. They find ways to hide or glaze over the seriousness of the problem, trusting that either it will just work itself out or someone else will deal with it. We move on to the next challenge, role, or business innovation. However, when too many deeply rooted problems are left unsolved or shoved to the side, business casualties (people, customers, market share, and new opportunities) occur.

The Business of Change—or Not?

Problem solving done the way it has been described here rarely leads to disruptive innovation. Our brains, our bodies, our teams, and our organizational systems are not set up to tear things down and create things at the same time. Each requires different ways of thinking and doing that are contrary to the way work happens and how people behave within these systems. We fall into these traps easily because our business systems are somewhere between the past and the future. The "go-to" models and mechanisms are steeped in tradition that worked well in a previous business environment under a different set of conditions. Given the pace of business and the rate of change today, the approaches summarized here are operational and business liabilities. In a recent article for *Harvard Business Review*, called "Accelerate!," author John Kotter put it this way: "An organization that's facing a real threat or eyeing a new opportunity tries—and fails—to cram through some sort of major transformation using a change process that worked in the past. But the old ways of setting and implementing strategy are failing us. We can't keep up with the pace of change, let alone get ahead of it." As people try to find real answers to produce better results, these outdated approaches are used at the expense of *real* solution creation. The challenge is to find new ways to understand and literally *see* the past while planning and strategizing for the future *at the same time*.

Are there really new ways to plan and strategize that won't cost a company a fortune? As we look back on the scenarios just described, there are several points where the inclusion of pictures

along with strong business models might have led to different results. In an era of tight budgets, layoffs, reorganizations, and sluggish to flat employment conditions, business suffers and cannot afford lavish and well-meaning strategy sessions that do not produce real results—only a nice picture. However, I argue that it's the people inside of these businesses, those who make the products and sell and deliver the goods and services, who really suffer. They suffer from lack of engagement and bad strategic processes that do not get cascaded into their workplace and have little to no relevance for them. The more employees suffer as a result of bad processes, poorly timed business changes, and lack of engagement, the more the overall business suffers. These persistent conditions create a downward spiral.

We wonder why overall productivity is down, and why 71 percent of the American workforce is either not engaged in or completely disengaged from their work. These workers are not fringe, "bad," or lazy. This is more than half the people employed in the United States. These are people who are motivated to contribute to a change or a product that will deliver value and improve the company. They want to save the company money. They want to feel that they are a part of solutions and improvements that contribute to the overall well-being of the organization. They can see ways to change. However, they do not have the right status or influence in the company to get heard. Management and leadership are often occupied by other things, so the gaps continue to grow in companies in the United States and around the world.

Business systems, structures, and cultures are averse to the changes that some people see and the changes that most companies need to make. Our large, complex multinational business systems are rooted in their history in the industrial age. While we have left the industrial age behind, our mindset, business patterns, and behaviors have not adapted to fit or meet the demands of a twenty-first-century marketplace. We call the leaders in our companies "chiefs," reflecting their role and the authority of a few to make decisions for many. It's hard to find ways and means of involving more people in critical or strategic decisions made by businesses. Frankly, the systems are unwieldy. Can business find new ways to engage more and more people without raising expectations and costs at the same time?

The silo mindset may have to be one of the first things to go. Sabina Spencer, business strategist and author, commented, "One of the biggest issues in almost every business today, is the predominance of *the silo mindset*. Whether it is by product, market, function, region, or nation, these separations are costly on many levels." Involving workers at all levels of the company in designing and participating in business and decision strategy has cost a lot of money and time, with mixed results. Taking people out of "production" to get a few good ideas has long been seen as a wasted investment. This is the industrial-age perspective, and from that vantage point, it makes sense. Will McInnes, cofounder and managing director of the online marketing and social consultancy company NixonMcInnes and author of *Culture Shock: A Handbook for 21st Century Business*, calls for a new perspective on engagement built out of demand and necessity: "Twenty-first century businesses demand much more from their leaders. This networked age, with workforces dispersed across different nations, working fluidly from various locations connected in new ways by digital tools, requires a different leadership approach. . . . Key to success as a leader in the 21st century are these values of collaboration, dialogue, transparency and authenticity—command and control just won't work anymore."

What do we have to do to succeed in the twenty-first century? And what are we willing to do in order to get there? Desperate times, while difficult to endure, often provide the catalyst for new ways of working. The desperate measures that some people are willing to take to achieve astonishing results have produced stories that are the legends of business school case studies (think Lou Gerstner [IBM], Jack Welch [GE], Fred Smith [FedEx], Sandy Weill [Citigroup], and Ray Anderson [Interface Inc.]). What makes their stories the stuff of legend is their willingness to rise above the fear of acting in an "unnatural" way to achieve something extraordinary. Acts of desperation and acts of courage typically fall into the same category when we hear about exceptional acts. What kind of courage will the business leaders of today need to have to push through the constraints that still bind us to the industrial age? Could the use of pictures with business strategy help to make this breakthrough profitable and energizing?

Many leaders, including myself, who have taken the risk to interweave business strategy with pictures would emphatically argue that this is one of the most important paths to take in the future. Sabina Spencer goes on to explain,

> The power of strategic illustration is that it encourages dialogue between the different parts of a company in such a way that the images captured help to identify areas where synergies can happen. People realize that they are not as separate as they thought, and they begin to see opportunities for higher levels of collaboration that can promote real innovation, reduce unnecessary duplication, and increase effectiveness.

They see the value in the different perspectives as the pictures of their connectedness emerge through the drawing. The beauty of the whole picture is that everyone's contribution is valued, not just the ones with the loudest voices or the highest pay grades! Hierarchy and power dynamics take a back seat as breakthrough thinking lifts the strategic conversation to *a one company* approach that usurps the traditional *us versus them* discussions that only perpetuate the status quo.

I have used this methodology with many clients, especially executive and leadership teams who are leading major corporations. Through the drawing of these metaphorical maps, the connections between the members are strengthened, and they start to place a higher value on the collective. It is a process that puts equal importance on both the task and the relationship side of the equation for creating successful brand identities, where employee and customer engagement are critical to the success of an enterprise.

Let's examine what happens when someone with leadership responsibilities has the vision, courage, and desperation to engage with her people around problem solving and planning for the future. When they are willing to deeply explore the problems and solutions of their division and create the space for new possibilities through the use of good business tools and pictures, the decisions they take and the results they can achieve can be transformative.

CHAPTER 2

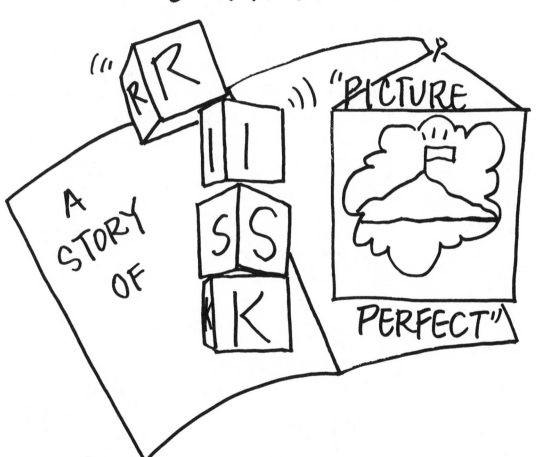

"RISK"

A STORY OF

"PICTURE PERFECT"

A newly appointed senior vice president, Sean, works for a growing multinational technology company based in London. Sean, who is ambitious and who has previously been successful, had been assigned to a business division that had once achieved double-digit growth and been the darling of the company. The division had once been known for creating innovative solutions with and for its customers, but its gross sales had fallen by 50 percent in the last year, and its customer base had eroded as those same customers adopted new technologies and products. "We're just not sure what happened there, Sean," the CEO confided. "We have confidence in your ability to get in there and clean it up. This could mean great things for you professionally."

As Sean studied the financial and marketing data, he saw that growth had been flat to nonexistent for more than two years. This came as a surprise to him. "Why did they let it go for so long?" he thought. When Sean went around the office and talked to the employees about the division's financial and product performance, he found them uninterested and tired.

When Sean asked the employees why they thought things had changed, they offered many reasons and compared today to the "good old days." None of these people were able to make direct eye contact with him. They blamed management, the economy, or fickle customers, but none of their

stories were the same. After a few months in the role, and with pressure building from the board of directors and the CEO, Sean knew no more about the problem than he had ideas about how to turn things around.

One night, Sean was having dinner with a close friend and professional colleague, Cheryl, whom he had worked with at another company. There they had developed great rapport and respect for one another. They recognized each other's ability and each felt that the other was able to see things that were unique to the problem. They trusted each other, and each valued the other's perspective. Sean told her of his dilemma in his current role. He talked about his frustration with the company for not having done anything to fix the problem for years. He complained about the employees, who seemed not to care and not to really understand the situation they were in. Exasperated, he wondered whether he and his team could fix the problem, even if the solution was right in front of them.

Cheryl looked at him with concern. She had not seen him this perplexed or frustrated in many years. He looked worried. "Have you slept at all?" she asked. "No," he stated bluntly. "I don't get it. What are they afraid of? I feel like I am being set up to fail." Cheryl took a deep breath and reached for her smartphone. She pulled up a picture on the phone. "What's this?" he asked.

"My division's new action plan." Sheepishly, Cheryl handed the phone to Sean.

He laughed. "You're kidding, right?"

"Actually, no." Cheryl went on to explain that big targets had been set for her team this year. Her group was not achieving its numbers. The group members knew that growth was happening in the market; customers were buying—just not her product. She and her team were stuck, but they could not figure out how they got there or how to get out of their situation. Together they had held several offsite strategy sessions and got nowhere.

A senior colleague in her business recommended a different approach. "Try using a business artist, graphic facilitator, strategic illustrator—whatever the person calls it. These people can help you really 'see' the problems. They draw what you say, when you say it, right in front of you. It gets everybody on the same page. The use of pictures helps all of you to see where and why you are stuck. It also helps you see what you can do in the future. It's kind of like magic, but it works. The people in my company use these strategic illustrators all the time." Cheryl finished, "It was kind of crazy. Everyone started seeing the same problems, and we all got on the same page. The guy drew things as we talked, and we saw what was holding us back. We had honest and candid conversations. Since then, I feel like everyone on the team is pulling in the same direction; everyone is engaged. I can't believe it myself, but we are motivated. We've made progress, and we constantly compare the results we have with what we designed on the large map—this mural thing. That's it on my phone." Cheryl pointed to the image. "I don't know, but what have you got to lose?" As they parted, Cheryl passed along the contact information of the strategic illustrator she had used. Skeptical, Sean thanked her. "Well, if you really think this sort of thing can help, I might try it."

"Okay, everyone—welcome, thank you for your time," Sean started, glancing at the guy behind him, who was using a green marker to write the word "welcome" on a large poster. "I am glad that everyone is here. I know it's been a while since the whole team has been together, and I am glad we are sitting around the same table now. I think this division's been stuck for a while, and we need a fresh way to look at a few problems. This is Daniel. He is a strategic illustrator and graphic facilitator. Daniel has worked with other businesses to support people like us as we try to think about the same old problems in new ways. He is going to capture our conversations over the rest of the day on big pieces of paper, and help facilitate the meeting so that I can participate. He will deliver a drawing to us that will outline our conversations, the decisions we make, and what outcomes we decide on."

Sean looked around at the people on his team. Eyes rolled: "Been here, done this." Other people thought, "What's Sean up to? Is he going to use all this information against us to get us fired?" And a few people in the room thought, "Well, this is going to be different. . . ." Sean's palms were sweating. He went on, "You had a chance to look at the agenda ahead of time, and I am looking forward to what we come up with."

Sean put a flipchart on the wall, and the team members were surprised by what they saw. "This is a guide for our work today. I want to know about the past, when you and this division were at your best. What were the keys to your success? And if we have to choose, what are some things from the past that we want to bring into the present and the future? Daniel is going to help us think about some ideas for the future."

Sean sat down with the group. "When we leave here today, I would like to have two or three actions that we think can help move us out of the hole we're in and set the stage for going forward. Does this sound reasonable?" As Sean proposes the outcomes, Daniel draws them on the wall.

Heads nodded. Of course they nod—he is the boss! He genuinely wondered what people were thinking. Daniel talked the team through the agenda, and the meeting began.

AGENDA

AT OUR BEST, WE...

KEYS TO SUCCESS?

WHAT SHOULD WE TAKE WITH US?

The team members began by talking about their past. Stories about the "good old days" were spun, and people's eyes lit up; they laughed and joked. It was as if Sean were not even there. They talked about some of the best conversations they had had with their customers, what it felt like to exceed budget projections, what it took to create innovative products and scale them for larger distribution channels. To Sean's surprise, he learned about a great leader the division had had five years ago that everyone had admired. They described him as a person who held them responsible for their work while letting them do what they needed to do in order to stay ahead of the market.

The group talked about the ideas that had worked and why. Daniel asked questions that helped to peel away some of the frustrations the employees were experiencing as a team. He captured everything they said with images, symbols, and words. As they worked on the future for the team, Daniel added images of people who felt pride and customers who offered solutions.

With each set of questions that Daniel posed, his drawing illuminated and portrayed what was holding the division back from attracting new customers and creating new products based on market demand. It became clear to everyone that what the team needed in the short term was to get out of its rut, and they reflected on what

they were going to do when they got back to the office. Sean participated in the conversations, but he sat back listening while other
people were taking the lead. The time flew by. By the end of the day,
the team members had a full-blown visual image of their next steps
and agreements on who would do what, by when. They even signed
the map along the bottom and set dates for their next set of meetings to track and follow up on their commitments and the actions
that needed to be taken.

When asked what would happen to the visual maps that had
been created, Sean stated, "We are going to have these digitally
scanned and sent to everyone here. What do you think about sharing

these maps with your team members? Should you tell them what happened and see what they think?" The group agreed, and Sean congratulated all of them for their work and thanked them for their time. People lingered in the room and the hallway, continuing their conversations.

Sean conferred with Daniel. "How did that go?" he asked. As they glanced around the room, they noticed that people had drawn their ideas on the notepads and on the backs of napkins. Daniel smiled. "I think it went well. At least we got them thinking." He said, pointing to the tables, "I think you did a great job of setting the tone and the expectations. Let's stay focused on the team's outcomes and see where you and the team end up."

Sean and Daniel checked in with each other and with the members of the senior team regularly to assess and reflect on how the division's work was progressing relative to what had been committed to on the map. Sean dropped in on a couple of meetings where the senior team was sharing the ideas that had initially been discussed at their off-site. The senior team met each week to talk about how things were going. Each time they met, they used the visual map to focus their conversations and discuss their progress. They used red pens to mark out what had been completed, and they began writing on the map, highlighting changes, challenges, or new information. A person on the team was able to add the changes directly to the digital versions of the map. The updated visual was sent out to all team members.

Sean could see that the morale of the senior team was improving. Even those who had been skeptical at the beginning of the offsite meeting were talking to Sean and consulting him on key decisions. Nevertheless, nothing was happening in terms of performance, meeting their financial and product targets, or improving their overall results. It felt as if they had peeled away the top layer of the problem, but they had not gotten down to the real business issue. Sean realized that his division needed to do more. The board and the CEO were putting that pressure on him regularly.

At the next meeting, Sean stated this reality to his senior team. He tried to be frank and candid, without judgment, but when he asked the team why it thought nothing had changed, the room went cold and silent. In spite of his effort to sound neutral, his frustration and disappointment came across clearly. A young woman, Valerie, who had been with the senior team for only a short time, looked directly at Sean and said, "We aren't there yet, and what we are doing is not good enough." Everyone stared at her and at Sean. "Valerie, can you say more about this?" Sean inquired. The room was still.

"This is complicated," Valerie started. "In the off-site, we were able to come together as a team, get clarity on some of the key issues, and agree on the next steps. We have made progress, and I think you can tell that from the morale of this group—it feels good to be doing something, having a plan." She continued, "The problem is that given the size and history of this division, there are so many people and processes to review, to take into account, and to consider. Everyone thinks he has the right answer, and I am still not sure I actually know what solution we are working on. Honestly, everyone in this room is trying to hold on to his people and their positions instead of really taking a risk in trying to solve many of the problems we face." Valerie paused, and mayhem broke loose. Talking over one another, people were frustrated; they disagreed, raised their voices, and appealed to Sean. Valerie sat quietly with her arms folded.

Sean tried to listen to all the different points of view regarding priorities and actions. "Hold on here. Stop! This is not the right way to go about discussing this," Sean said. As people quieted, he said, "You are all correct. You all have some form of the right answer. We need more clarity on what we can do to change and what is holding us back. Would you be open to another session with Daniel? Maybe if we map it, we can see it." People looked around at each other.

Charlie, the manager of one of the largest groups in the division, who had strong opinions about everything, challenged Sean. "I think we should do that again with everyone in the room, the whole division." Sean felt as if he were being tested. Charlie continued, "That drawing was like a map, a guide we could use to get all the ideas in one place. I think we need more ideas than what we have here in this group. We are too close to the information, and Valerie is right—we all are protecting our turf and our teams. I think my team would appreciate being part of something like this, don't you? Everyone has seen the first map we created, and they are curious about the process, about how we got those specific images and actions. The reaction of the people on my team to the maps has been positive; they are curious. I think our people see things that we can't see. I know they see things differently. Who knows? We might get some new ideas to build on and get everyone involved."

Sean considered. This was an expensive and potentially time-consuming investment. He wondered whether it would produce any results. How smart would it be for him and his career to hold this big meeting with everyone in the company knowing about it?

The lack of performance was a strong concern of top management, and they had threatened to lay off people from his division. What could something like this produce? He sat back and remembered his conversation with Cheryl. He recalled her amazement at the speed with which her division had been able to turn things around.

Sean turned to his team. "I can't do this without you. If we do this, we all have to be in it together. Everyone on this team has to take a leadership role in the planning and delivery. We all have to be committed to getting the best possible outcome in the least amount of time—in one day." By the end of the meeting, everyone was in agreement. They would move forward.

The members of the senior team really pulled together. They worked together on the agenda. They invited Daniel to work with them on some graphical images that would spark specific conversations and lead the division in the creation of a picture of future performance and product outcomes. The senior team took ownership

of the meeting, consulting with Sean, Daniel, and other key employees. What was their focus? To create a new future for the division. How did they plan to do it? With *pictures*.

On the day of the divisionwide meeting, Sean was nervous and
excited. Daniel was ready to draw and to step in when they needed
someone from the outside to help move the process along. There
was a certain buzz in the room, too. He noticed that hanging up
around the meeting space were several black-and-white flipchart-
size sheets of paper with words on them in colored markers. The
template looked like this:

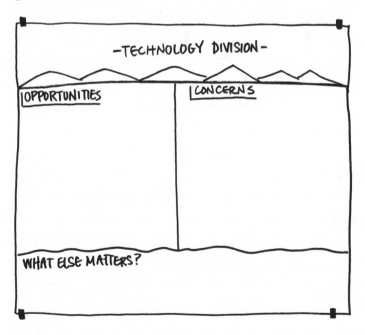

People walked into the room, chatting and laughing. The group looked far different from the group he had started working with a few months ago. People made a point of looking at the templates hanging on the wall. After Sean's welcome to the division, the focus of the meeting was clearly stated: create a new future for the division. Questions were posed by the senior team, and people at the small tables set to work.

Sean walked around the room and listened to the conversations, he looked at the content on the flipchart templates, and he began to see and hear patterns. The way people talked about themselves and their work was consistent. Many of the conversations revealed the key things that were holding the division back. These key things came up again and again, and Daniel captured them on the large sheet of paper at the front of the room. As the session moved into the afternoon, the plan for the division became clear. It was visualized; people were committed to actions and timelines.

Functional groups planned to work together on specific actions and had agreed to aggressive targets. Sean was amazed at the energy, enthusiasm, and excitement that he saw. This was a completely different group of people to work with. They were colleagues who were working with him and with one another to achieve a goal.

As people left the meeting, they thanked Sean for taking the time that allowed them to "be part of the solution," "create the future," and "be here." Daniel shook Sean's hand, congratulating him. "Well done. Now, watch out—and don't get in their way, " he said, smiling. "I think you are going to get what you want."

You can imagine how the story ends—actually, it doesn't end. This was just the beginning. And the map lived on within the business. The division creatively reinvented itself to earn the respect and positive attention of the board of directors. The team members showed the board the map. They were allowed more space and time to develop their strategy and to go after new customers in new markets. The senior team was clear about where the division was headed and what performance indicators would be used to measure their success. The senior team worked across the division to ensure that everyone made the targets. The hand-drawn visuals became a regular part of their work and practice. When people got lost, they referred to the map; when they were confused, they used the map for direction; when someone new joined the team, they showed her the map. Several times, when they needed to make changes or wanted something a bit more professional than what

they could produce, they brought in Daniel or one of his colleagues. The way people in the division thought and worked had an impact throughout the company. As employees left Sean's division and were promoted to new roles in different parts of the company, they took their map, their story, and their success with them.

Many clients, customers, colleagues, and business leaders have cast a skeptical eye on the use of pictures to transform business strategies and decisions. Before we look at the specifics that helped to transform Sean's team, it's important to provide both additional background grounded in research and context concerning the use of pictures, images, and metaphors in business transformation.

CHAPTER 3

HOW PICTURES TRANSFORM BUSINESS

The field of strategic illustration, graphic recording, graphic facilitation, and visual facilitation is relatively new. It began in the San Francisco Bay area in the 1970s and quickly migrated to cities like Toledo, Ohio, and Manhattan with different thinking and approaches. A series of artists, business leaders, and entrepreneurs wondered whether there was a better way to get more out of the meetings they led or were a part of. In meetings with customers, their teams, and others, they began to experiment with combining the use of pictures with business processes, such as SWOT (strengths, weaknesses, opportunities, and threats) analysis. Early risk takers and leaders in the field include David Sibbet (president of the Grove Consultants International, one of the "founders" of the concept Group Graphics™ with Geoff Ball and Fred Lakin and author of *Visual Meetings*, 2010, *Visual Leaders*, 2013, and numerous articles, blogs, and posts), Nancy Margulies (author and artist of *Yes, You Can . . . Draw!*, 1991, *Mapping Inner Space*, 2001, and *Visual Thinking* with Christine Valenza, 2005), and Geoff Ball. Nancy White, Susan Kelly, Michael Doyle, and David Straus (authors of *How to Make Meetings Work*, 1976), and Bill Hinsch (Learning Visuals) contributed unique styles and processes with business visuals as more businesses adopted this practice. These and other innovators pushed the boundaries of what was perceived as "acceptable" in internal business processes. Their pictures, images, and words were aimed at the heart of the organizations they worked with, not at the marketing or commercial side of the business.

In their meetings, they would help direct and focus their groups while recording, capturing, and visualizing them. Their experiments grew in scope and scale until these leaders could easily engage whole companies in relevant business conversations while creating colorful, large-scale "maps" of the conversations, the strategies, the focus, and the commitments of those present.

What do strategic illustrations actually do? In contrast to works of fine art that we see in museums, strategic illustrations and graphic recordings employ practical, everyday, and familiar icons, colors, and words to give meaning to our ideas, struggles, and opportunities. The images may often be crude and even elementary, but they convey and make a clear point, and they capture a concept that has meaning in the context of business conversations and strategy sessions. In the same way that a street map or travel guide can help us find our way, strategic illustrations first and foremost orient people to where they are. They define our metaphorical landscape. This is both the real and the perceived landscape in which we work. The real landscape includes the physical workplace, our division, our coworkers located in other communities and on other continents, and the large-scale systems like multinational businesses and governments. The perceived landscape can be a company mindset, internal politics and processes, organizational structure, norms of decision making, and any other factors that affect the business decisions that are made. A synthesis of both landscapes allows a team or stakeholders to see and understand factors that are unique to their

distinct "landscape." The pictures used often capture the shared history of the organization and explain how the business arrived at its current moment in history. Like the streets, landmarks, and intersections on a map, the images and words in a strategic illustration offer a way to review and discuss the "routes" taken, the twists and turns the organization has made. The illustration inspires the group members to reflect on why they traveled a specific route and what was gained (or lost) by that choice. Strategic illustrations provide a blank canvas where a new "landscape" can be created, including pictures of activities, products, and customers of the present and future.

STRATEGIC ILLUSTRATION

In October of 2008, I was teaching a graphic recording class in Paris. I was working with colleagues Pierre Goirand, Clydette de Groot, and Elizabeth Auzan, and our first class in Paris included students from the United States, the United Kingdom, France, Germany, and Brussels. The class offered them a wonderful opportunity to put their new drawing skills to work at the 10-year anniversary of the French Society for Organizational Learning (SoL) Conference. Nine of us from different backgrounds, cultures, and languages illustrated the conversations, discussions, and keynote presentations.

At a break, a group of us were discussing the experience with others from all over Europe. When I asked what they called this practice (in their own language), the French responded, "graphique recording," and others responded similarly. When I asked what they would call it besides a localized version of the American term *graphic recording*, they explained that "-ing" does not translate easily into other Latin languages. We were stumped. We explored various options, but we finally settled on "strategic illustration." Based on what we collectively knew and had experienced with businesses and business leaders, these two words could translate easily into their native language without sounding American. Strategic illustration also came the closest to describing the ultimate goal: to strategically visualize what businesses needed and wanted in order to grow. Thus the term *strategic illustration* was coined!

It's easy to read a map and still be lost. Like a location finder on a smartphone application or a GPS system, strategic illustrations can pinpoint our location, showing us where we are today and providing a picture of a "reality" that the group creates. Through the use of relevant questions about the business and a few reliable business models, images and pictures will home in on the activities that a team is performing. The full picture will tell more about why things are working and what to eliminate than a company survey or questionnaire and take less time. This pinpointing is a quick and speedy way for a team to get on the same page as it faces new opportunities or unexpected challenges.

Pictures also synthesize a set of activities or words into one image, as opposed to making a list of what we think, what people have said, or a conjecture as to what we believe other people think. Pictures say a great deal about one issue. We pinpoint it and at the same time give it texture, dimension, and even feelings, which is what we experience in life. For example, in Sean's story in Chapter 2, we had an image that showed two people with their heads down. What happens when a single word is added? Just adding the word "customer" to this image conveys so much more about how your customers feel than making a list about what you think.

CUSTOMER

Pinpointing with the use of an image can actually picture a problem in the system without giving it a specific name (one or two words that mean something to some people on a team and nothing to others). When we use pictures, we think of all the things a picture means or conveys. We do not spend time trying to agree on the "right" word to describe the situation or condition. Everything we need to know about the situation is there, in one image. A picture may actually move a team to talk more deeply about whatever is pictured, like the customer. For example, I have seen groups look at an image similar to that of the customer portrayed and immediately begin discussing what they can do to improve and change that image to show what they *want* the customer to look like compared to what they see now. How can such a simple and quick visual image and process deliver this level of clarity and insight?

As strategic illustrations are developed and people share information, individual data become group data. As we watch the strategic illustrator incorporate the different views that we hear, we begin to incorporate what we hear and see into our thinking as well. As the group's picture of itself changes with the view emerging on the map, so does an individual's picture of himself change. The map can actually shift people's view from one perspective or position to another just by the simple inclusion of everyone's ideas. People in the group can use the pictures, as containers of ideas, to form new

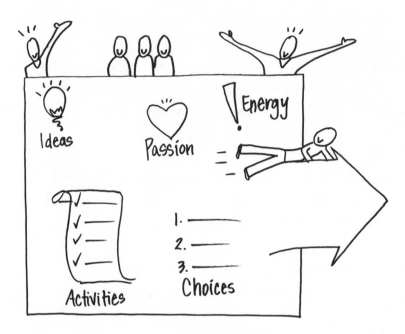

agreements about what to use and do. Teams see the choices that fit with their business focus, and they align with those choices almost immediately. Their energy and focus move in that direction because they helped to create the goal.

Have you ever seen maps on the sidewalks in big cities that say, "You Are Here"? Tourists and locals can see where they are in relation to where they want to go. Strategic illustrations are used in the same way. We hang them in our hallways; we print and duplicate them; we e-mail them or post them to websites. We use them over and over again to see where we are relative to where we want to be.

These images show us, at a glance, how to close the distance between where we are as a team and where we need to be. At a glance, the team knows where it is headed and why.

In the newspaper *Consensus*, Geoff Ball summarized it like this: "Graphic facilitation supports the resolution of conflicts by going beyond a solely verbal approach. Graphic facilitation helps manage the complexity of group discussions. It reflects back the expression of multiple perspectives, makes connections between thoughts, provides a way to store information, describes a complex flow of activity, energizes a group, helps a group maintain sufficient focus to work together, and provides an explicit structure for thinking."

A RELEVANT TOOL FOR BUSINESS TRANSFORMATION

The best data available about the use of visuals to improve retention and enhance learning in a complex world are in the field of visual literacy. John Debes, cofounder of the International Visual Literacy Association, coined the phrase in 1969 and described it in this way: "Visual Literacy refers to a group of vision-competencies a human being can develop by seeing and at the same time having and integrating other sensory experiences. The development of these competencies is fundamental to normal human learning. When developed, they enable a visually literate person to discriminate and interpret the visible actions, objects, symbols, natural or man-made, that he encounters in his environment. Through the creative use of these competencies, he is able to communicate with others."

The research on visual literacy has focused primarily on young people and their early learning years. The extensive (and somewhat disaggregated) body of research documents reveals how and why young people learn more, retain more, and do it more quickly through the explicit use of visuals. You can find examples of the research used for this book in the Bibliography. While the reading and deductions about young people are compelling, can we say that the same process works for adults?

As discussed in Chapter 1, as children, we all begin by thinking visually. The research into visual literacy does not translate extensively into adult learning, so we turn to brain science and cognitive research to help us understand that this works and why. Jackie Andrade, a researcher at the University of Plymouth, showed "that doodlers actually remember more than nondoodlers when asked to retain tediously delivered information, like, say, during a boring meeting or a lecture." Upon further examination, Andrade and her team found that doodling actually prevents daydreaming, which distracts the brain's ability to focus. Daydreaming, it turns out, requires a lot of the brain's processing power. The study concludes that "doodling forces your brain to expend just enough energy to stop it from daydreaming but not so much that you don't pay attention."

The fine line between attention and daydreaming can make the difference between retention and motivation for many people, especially in teams and organizations that are beleaguered by too many boring strategy or planning sessions that yield little results.

From cognitive and brain research, we know that when adults use doodling, drawing, and business visuals, this engages both the right and the left sides of the brain. Up until 10 years ago, the science about how the right brain and the left brain worked was fairly static. In nonmedical terms, we knew that the left brain was all business—analytical, rational, linear, and organized. Left-brain thinking belonged to accountants, lawyers, doctors, and business leaders— successful people. In their roles, who needed the right brain?

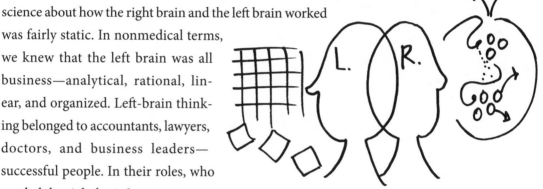

Traditionally, the right brain has long been associated with intuition, relationships, seeing systems, randomness, chaos, creativity, and nonlinear thinking. Artists, musicians, and "creative types" had a use for this part of the brain. Maybe people in marketing and sales needed a bit of right-brain thinking in the business environment because their jobs are, after all, partially creative. Our collective thinking was fairly consistent on this "fact." For some of us, early in our education, we were actually divided into students who were "creative" and those who were "more serious."

LEFT   RIGHT

We now know that there are important external stimuli that encourage the two sides of the brain to work together. Three of these stimuli are art, music, and mathematics. When the brain is engaged in listening to, thinking deeply about, or actually doing math, art, or music, our neural synapses "fire" across the two sides of the brain. Art and music promote brain elasticity, support better cognitive function, help with retention of information in all subject areas, and influence learning abilities later in life.

Previously, we envisioned the two sides of the brain as working independent of each other. We now know that the two sides of the brain work together. In an update to previous research, Miriam Vered reports, "Visual imagery is another example [of how the left and the right brain work together simultaneously]. In the popular perspective, [visual imagery is] a right brain function. But fascinating experiments have shown that specific areas in both left and right brain are in fact crucial [to full cognitive function]. Brain imaging studies of normal adults have shown activity in both hemispheres." Randomness, relationships, and systems from the right brain get

Our Dancing Brain

organized in ways that we can understand and make meaning of with the linear, systematic left side of the brain. New connections, possibilities, and ideas that germinate in left-brain thinking actually make sense in the way the right side of the brain organizes information. This and other research support new ways of thinking, working, and potentially doing business.

In addition, the central parts of the brain support left- and right-brain interaction. The prefrontal cortex (the front part of our brain) "is involved in thinking about the future, making plans, and taking action." The limbic system (deep in the center part of the brain) is "functionally related neural structures in the brain that are involved in emotional behavior." The entire complex neural system in each person's brain allows us to see patterns, imagine the future, emotionally react, and then rationalize our decisions based on what we see, feel, and know.

When someone is in the room drawing, when we are drawing, or when we draw with others, our body and brain engage on many levels. We are visually, physically (the pen, marker, or pencil in hand), and psychologically (with the content and context) involved. We can hear the pen against the paper, and we can see what we draw. The content may 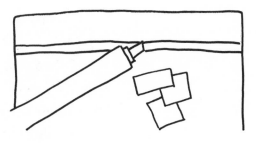 provoke some type of emotion (engaging the limbic system). This places extraordinary demands on many aspects of our brain to

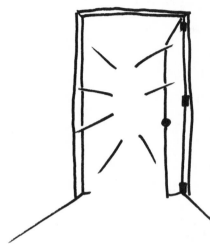

work together, process information, and make meaning. The amazing thing is that our brains deliver! We engage using multiple senses; we think, we wonder, we copy, and we doodle. Drawing is a bit like a door opener. We start thinking in ways that are different from the way we think when we use a spreadsheet, read something that is written on a page, or listen to a presentation. The multi-dimensional way in which we all think, sense, and see can be captured in a drawing. This allows us to relate to our colleagues and the ideas they have in new and exciting ways. Instead of focusing on one answer or one problem, when our brains are engaged with a drawing, they work in a multidimensional way that encourages us to think and be curious about multiple solutions to the problem or the challenge—not just one. This is solution creation in action. And, it happens when we or someone else draws!

This kind of collective breakthrough in teams and in business holds great promise for innovation and business growth. When we hear the early stories about Bill Gates and Steven Ballmer at Microsoft and Steve Jobs at Apple, we admire their "outside-the-box" thinking, their determination, and their creativity. They worked hard, and they had a vision of what they wanted to do. They saw the difference that their ideas could make and what those ideas could accomplish. These men used many aspects of their brains to help

them imagine and create things that had not been done or created before. They used tools, conversations, and images to
stimulate left- and right-brain interaction, and they
called upon the limbic system to direct and guide
their work. Were they aware of what their brains
were doing? Did they intentionally go about "working differently"? Their stories tell us yes. Is this kind
of synthesized, multidimensional approach available to only a few? Hardly. As we have just explored,
our brains are no different from theirs. The difference is having the courage to work with others in
new ways.

In the next chapter, let's have a look at Sean's story
and see how he and his team used pictures and images to unlock
the door to business possibilities.

CHAPTER 4

PICTURING YOUR BUSINESS STRATEGY IN 1½ ACTS

PICTURE THE OUTCOME

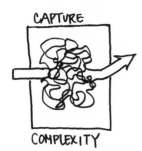

CAPTURE COMPLEXITY

CREATE POSSIBILITES

What happened to Sean and his team in Chapter 2 is not rocket science, nor is it unique. Turning a business around usually requires good leadership, focus, direction, persistence, planning, and a lot of hard work. What is unique in this situation is *how* Sean and his team went about doing the work.

There are three simple principles at work that can ensure that pictures support any business strategy as it emerges, regardless of the models or approaches used to create the strategy. Pictures combined with these principles can simplify, clarify, and help prioritize direction, action, and possibilities in less time for less money, with incredible results.

The three principles are:

> Picture the outcome
>
> Capture complexity
>
> Create possibilities

In the next three sections, Sean's story will be used to set the stage and explain each of the three principles. The key features of each principle will be combined with insights and perspectives from practitioners, clients, and customers as well as visual images to help you remember the features. The goal is to make each principle memorable and easy to use so that you can use it immediately in the business environment. After a little practice and experimentation, teams will find themselves using these principles as a way to visually and operationally structure and organize their work. They are the essential tools used to picture your business strategy.

ACT ONE: PICTURE THE OUTCOME

As Sean started his quest for solutions for his business division, he had an *idea* of what he wanted to accomplish with his team and his division. While he could not fully see the outcome, given his experience in the company, he trusted himself to be able to get to an outcome. By using the insights and experience of the people in his division and assistance from Daniel, the division created a vision of its future that the people in it could see, identified the appropriate activities to get going, and counted on the picture changing as they progressed. Armed with a picture that everyone shared, they began the hard work of rebuilding the division and creating new possibilities.

In any business strategy development process, picturing the outcome is one of the best places to begin. Doing so provides the team with focus and a clear direction. Everyone on the team sees his role and his responsibilities and has agreed to goals that often underpin the outcome. When there are multiple stakeholders involved, creating images of individual and organizational outcomes helps with alignment, clarification, and success management. Pictures of a complex project can be used to allow team members to check in

Best possible
Outcome

Target
Customer

Integrated
Systems

Operational
Strategies

Leadership Communication

Stakeholder Support

regularly, making sure that they are on course and following through on what was essentially agreed to initially. Oversight and course correction become easier, because if you can see something that needs to change—if it's not on the map—you simply change it.

An example of this occurred with a client while we were in a discussion about a complex information technology (IT) change. The system and process changes were being launched in 12 countries around the world, and the project involved people from the business, research, product development, sales, and operations areas. It also included people in different time zones who spoke multiple languages and came from different cultures. The IT product was an important change for the company, and there were many stakeholders to engage, educate, and communicate the changes to. When I asked my client, "What is the best possible outcome for you and for this project?," she began describing a system that was simple, that was integrated, and that gave results that were different from what the company had today. Her map ended up looking something like a pyramid. As we focused on specific details related to her desired outcomes, it became clear to her who the key customer was in this change process. She began to imagine the critical communication vehicles that were required and the specific operational strategies that were needed to ensure that all parts of the system would be able to fully benefit from the new changes. Trusting in the combined knowledge of the people in the business and their relationships with the stakeholders, she could see how what she imagined would actually work among all involved and would help achieve the desired effect. She saw it in one picture that she helped to draw. She took the image back to her project team, and the team used it to cascade the actions, benchmarks, and timeline required.

Imagination is a good thing. From a "neuroscientific point of view, imagining an act and doing it are not as different as they sound." Norman Doidge, M.D. (author of *The Brain That Changes Itself*), shares how the same part of the brain is activated when people are taking action and when they are imagining an action. "That is why visualizing can improve performance," he claims. From a brain science perspective, the prefrontal cortex, the home of the imagination, helps an individual see things beyond what is possible at present. The limbic system, the home of intuition, provides the "gut check" needed to test what is imagined for reality and relevance. Clearly, pictures are one of the few media that adequately capture both *imagination* and *intuition* when it comes to the connection between doing an action and imagining that action. The most successful results are those that people have "seen" (that is, have imagined and felt), then made happen. A picture provides a framework that we can

use to test assumptions and rationalize changes while still stretching beyond what is present and real today.

Doidge refers to this activity as "mental practice." It's the same thing that athletes or musicians do to get ready for a competition, a performance, or a big event. They imagine themselves in every possible condition or situation, and their acquired skill, knowledge, and ability pull them through. They see themselves performing with ease and grace. The result is excellence at its finest. The mental practice of repeating this over and over produces winning results.

This activity is not the exclusive domain of musicians or athletes. Employees, business owners, and leaders can use this same strategy to envision and picture an outcome for the business. This vision begins to take shape as different aspects of a solution, a product, a service, or a process are discussed, worked, and reworked in the mind and among groups. Using the experience and knowledge of all involved, the possibilities are explored, including risks and rewards. Like athletes, people and teams get clear about what picture they have created. They rehearse the outcome in their minds and in their conversations. The "picture" (the vision) of a future action or activity is compelling, it has meaning, and it is something in which that team or individual belongs. The picture becomes part of the people themselves.

Before locking in on a specific outcome, it is important that you share, discuss, and socialize (for example, talk about) your ideas with others beyond your team. A richer picture of what's possible is created based on the comments, questions, and contributions related to the picture that you have created. It is easy to get caught up in the energy of the process and think, "Yeah! This is it! We got it right!" Not so fast. Getting attached to or locked into an outcome and a picture can actually limit buy-in and diminish the learning that comes from consulting with others and sharing the picture and the outcomes with them. By fixating on one way of seeing the picture, you and the team may prevent others from sharing their connections and insights. They may believe that you have thought through everything and that you are asking for their input after the fact. A team that is attached to its outcome ends up defending its position, selling its picture to others, and explaining a great deal about the picture to others before you share it with them to make sure that they "get it right."

One of the net benefits of sharing an incomplete picture with a loosely formed outcome is the collective intelligence that is gathered. The intelligence that is gleaned from the sharing sessions ultimately changes the picture, but it can also end up changing the system you work in. Clients have indicated that the collective intelligence they have gathered during a sharing session has yielded "missing information," "details that were overlooked," "new strategies and opportunities that were never seen before," and "quick wins" toward the outcome. The point of having a business strategy in pictures is to create something with your team and others with whom you work, not to present a "final result" of strategy, actions, and outcomes. The results are very different. Here is an example.

While I was working with a successful technology firm in London, the sales team envisioned a new way to interact with the firm's top 25 clients. The sales team was frustrated by the lack of attention that its very successful online product was receiving from key decision makers within these top 25 companies. A series of mapping sessions and discussions with the sales team revealed that the senior executives who make marketing investment decisions were not in the room when the sales team made its pitch for online investments. The very people who had the resources to invest more in online marketing were clueless as to the effectiveness of the firm's online product. The team pictured an outcome where these same senior-level executives had a "visual experience" in which both the client and the sales team could see the online product as a direct way to increase overall sales. As the sales team began to visually map out the experience they wanted to have with the senior executives, the ultimate goal became clear: to increase annual sales with the top 25 clients by 20 percent. The way the team members planned to do this was through the cocreation of a strategy that uniquely engaged and inspired both businesses in delivering the end result.

In the end, a large-scale customized visual template was designed, along with an easy-to-use process for all sales and account managers to use to lead with their most exclusive clients. The sessions themselves were quick—only 90 minutes. The sales team and account managers used a specific set of questions in each session that allowed everyone in the room to explore how to improve the relationship between the two firms, increase profits, and share ideas about what each party was willing to do to make that happen. They captured the conversations and commitments using the visual template in colors signifying actions. Through this simple, rapid, and highly engaging process, the client easily hit its target of a 20 percent sales increase. The team also created new relationships with senior executives that engaged multiple levels of the business—technical, sales, marketing, and business strategy—as its approach was unique and productive. Everyone across the client's supply chain wanted to be engaged in the process.

Sabine Soeder, business consultant, strategic illustrator, and lighting architect from Dresden, Germany, reflected about the effectiveness of pictures and a cocreated strategy when she said, "Visuals are a great tool to support communication, to build bridges to understand each other, to make the complex visible and/or tangible, and to mirror what is. Different aspects of the organization and the process include people's perspectives, their ideas, and their vision. People have a chance to 'see' it all—the process and the ideas as well as the conversations. They understand them and can more easily make decisions that lead to actions and results."

Talking and sharing information about what is happening in the business is real life. It can happen covertly (at the watercooler) or overtly (through a formal "town hall"–style meeting). Using an informal and conversational approach allows colleagues to see the picture, imagine the outcome, and then contribute ideas and insights that may not have been part of the initial thinking. Some of the nuances and subtleties between and within organizational systems, reporting structures, and the company culture are pulled forward into the picture as teams and outsiders talk with one another about them. The picture of the outcome becomes more accurate and real as more people talk about it.

As we socialize the outcomes imagined and colleagues share what they think about what they see, leaders and others on the team begin to see the organization through the eyes of the people we manage, the people who work for and with us. Leaders and team members often notice patterns, feedback loops, and gaps in the system that we did not see before. Why? The saying "A picture is worth a thousand words" is true; images mean different things to different people. In an organizational context, pictures often reflect the activities in the organization that are occurring at the same time, including competing priorities, conflicting directions, and confusion. Ideas are represented, every contribution is "right," and everything that is said and contributed matters.

Since there is no right or wrong interpretation of a picture, there is no "wordsmithing" and no arguments about what certain words mean. A consensus around a picture helps to lay a foundation for alignment that is the beginning of team and organizational success. This is particularly true in a multicultural environment where people can move through their discomfort with the language and not "getting it right" by discussing what they see in a metaphor or an image that is relevant to the business. These discussions are insightful and again use a conversational approach rather than a presentation. The discussion builds the path to deep and profound solution creation through consensus, agreement, and alignment. At the end of the day, it is easier to get a group of people to agree on an image than it is to get them to agree on a written document.

Imagining and sharing pictures of outcome(s) are also liberating. In his book *Strategic Vision Work*, strategist Ulric Rudebeck comments, "Now is the time to let the team members have the freedom to use their imagination. The work with pictures and images gives that freedom. Intuition, creativity and feelings reduce the risk of getting stuck about details and choice of words." The freedom and

creativity described allow for not only new ways of thinking, but also new energy concerning how and what we think about the future. This energy and momentum is part of the collective process, and it is what fuels the next stages: planning and executing the outcome.

Pictures create a mental and physical framework for an outcome, and they are incredibly powerful for individuals and organizations when they are shared. Individually, pictures show what is desired with an eye toward what is believed, what is feasible, and why. As each person becomes a stakeholder in the picture, he anchors into and focuses on what is next for him personally. Team members and employees leverage their own "mental practice" as they ask about, look at, and reflect on an outcome that is portrayed in images. They may see the ideas that they contributed to the picture, or they may gravitate toward the ideas that have meaning for them. Given that this is a picture and not a letter, contract, or report, individuals can quickly examine it, synthesize what was covered, and discern how they personally fit into it.

For the organization, seeing, understanding, and clarifying the outcome are critical. This clarity serves as a rudder, a guide, a "north star" in the middle of the complex systems, tense relationships, competitive pressures, and power struggles that prevail in all businesses.

From leaders to entry-level employees, everyone is looking for the direction in which the business is headed, an explanation of why it's headed in that direction, and what the plan for getting there is. The whole idea behind a "north star" is that everyone in the organization, regardless of where she sits, can see it. As previously mentioned, there is clarity about what the team is working toward and what is needed to get there.

In the end, businesses succeed when all their employees are engaged in some piece of the delivery. If you want people to be engaged in an outcome, you must let them share in the building and design of that outcome. This may require changing and morphing the original picture that you imagined. If so, expect employees and teams to be grateful and to appreciate the invitation to be part of the process. Employees who see themselves as part of the big picture are more likely to work toward that picture, not just do what someone tells them to do. While picturing your outcome sounds easy and straightforward, this still does not happen in many companies around the world today.

One final note on picturing the outcome: embedded in the demanding environments in which we work, there is a pressure to create the "right outcome" and to do it *immediately*. Given the ever-changing marketplace and environments that we live and work in, believing that anyone can create the "right outcome" from the beginning is unwise and fraught with failure. *Harvard Business Review* is full of case studies about businesses that created or stayed with a "solution" that they thought the world wanted. The final result was that the solution was rejected, or the world changed and their product or service did not. In the twenty-first century, a business's ability to be agile and responsive is key. The success of any organization is based on its ability to anticipate a customer's need, meet that need at the right time and at the right scale, and adapt as needed. You, your team, and your business need to allow a pictured outcome to morph and change in exactly the same way. As you and your team get closer to understanding what really matters to your customers, your people, and the business, your outcome will change. This is okay; in fact, it is actually a key to success. There is no such thing as an easy formula to get to the right outcome. In a fast-paced and changing environment, some tricks to remember are:

- Trust your knowledge. You are in your role and position with the company because of what you know and what you have done.

- Rely on your background, experiences, and relationships. They provide a wealth of resources that you can call on to test and course-correct your outcome when and as you need to.

- Tap into the knowledge of others who work with you and those who don't. Different perspectives can help you determine what elements of your outcome might change and what will stay the same.

- Share your picture of what the outcome could be with as many people as you can. This will allow you to focus and change in the same breath.

- Don't be afraid to change the outcome when you have good evidence, data, and reason to support the change. It's usually the market talking.

When you create a picture of the outcome, it is a catalyst for other things. Creating a shared picture of an outcome can transform a dull and depressed team into an engaged and motivated one by the simple inclusion of the team members' ideas. Your picture also provides critical focus and direction that keeps everyone on course, knowing what she needs to do, by when, and why. As a summary of key aspects of picturing the outcome:

1. Create a picture of the outcome. Trust yourself and your ideas.

2. Tap into your imagination and intuition to test your assumptions and ground your ideas.

3. Discuss your picture with other members of your team and your organization to get a richer picture of what they see as possible outcomes.

4. Build the foundation for alignment and agreement using a picture of your ideas, outcome, and strategies.

5. Don't get too attached to the outcome that you visualize or believe that there is a "right outcome." Instead, listen for patterns, challenges, and other conditions in the system that might get in the way of your success.

6. Don't be afraid of changing your outcome based on new information from peers or colleagues, the market, or data that make the case for change.

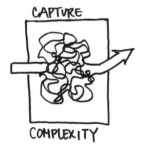

ACT TWO: CAPTURE COMPLEXITY

While Sean and his team were creating a series of outcomes and taking action on them using their map, they were also gathering complex information about the division. As the whole division engaged in the process, more of the complexities were revealed, and Sean began to see the patterns and performance behaviors that had led to the division's difficulties. His view of the business expanded as he learned more about it and as the layers of complexity expanded. He observed the political, operational, and functional challenges and inconsistencies, but he was not sure what to do with them. Others within the division also "saw" the complexities because Daniel had physically captured those complexities on a map. As the teams and individuals took in the complex picture of their world, the perceptions they had had about their division and their work changed. Somehow, the complexities became manageable and no longer inhibited focus and action. The whole division was able to prioritize. People knew what they had to focus on in order to achieve their goals. Complexity is at the center of Sean's story in the same way that it is at the center of almost every business today.

The layers of complexity that we experience in the workplace often tear us away from innovation and force us into bureaucracy and a level of detail that we don't understand (or care about). We are confused by what people want and what we want from them. With one foot in the industrial age and another in the future, we try to understand the past, present, and future all in the same breath.

Across industries, leaders and their teams balance external influences and new opportunities with the day-to-day management and oversight that deliver value. This creates a business environment that is unsettling at best, and in some cases terrifying. In John Kotter's *Harvard Business Review* article "Accelerate!," he notes, "The hierarchical structures and organizational processes we have used for decades to run and improve our enterprises are no longer up to the task of winning in the faster-moving world. In fact, they can actually thwart attempts to compete in a marketplace where discontinuities are more frequent and innovators must always be ready to face new problems."

Leaders and their teams need a quick and simple way to rise above the complexity that allows them to be both strategic and operational at the same time. Too often, managers fail to see the connections and conditions that contribute to success and at the same time process the details needed to make success happen. Business decisions that are made today have an impact on tomorrow's performance, and with so much confusion, contradiction, and complexity, how do we know what's "true"? How can we tell what is relevant to the business today and what isn't? There is a clear and obvious gap between the things that teams and their leaders perceive as being right or wrong and what is the actual reality. I call this predicament the *perception-reality gap*."

Perceptions include the stories and myths that circulate at watercoolers and from seasoned to new employees. Perceptions also include assumptions or expectations that are held, but that never get articulated or discussed. Doesn't everyone see and experience the same things at work? No, they don't. Individuals do not see and experience the same thing, and neither do teams. Each of us creates his own realities every moment of every day. This is the great thing about being human, and we all do it.

Perception is a part of how humans biologically survive. Our most basic and sophisticated biological systems ensure that we can survive in almost any environment, conditions, or circumstances. Using a network of neurons, our brain sends messages telling us to do what is required by the situation—solve a problem, create, strategize, plan, avoid, run, or freeze. These actions ensure individual survival. Part of the evolutionary strategy involving survival is our brain's ability to sort and prioritize data, and to dump those that are not important for or relevant to our survival. Each person's ability to do that is unique. Some of that sorting ability is chemical, some of it is environmental, and most of it is informed by how each person grows up. What each of us learned about "the world" as a child informs how she sees and experiences that world. This sorting and processing happens a million times a day in ways that we are hardly aware of. This brain function prioritizes what data we think are important and what we choose to focus on. The ability to sort and dump protects us physically and mentally. Physically, we can choose to run away or to fight whatever might be "attacking" us based on the messages that the brain receives, processes, and sends. Mentally, our brains find ways to make sense of the input and messages we receive that help us manage the feelings of being overwhelmed, exuberant, afraid, nervous, or scared.

Each person does this, with few exceptions (autistic people have slightly different challenges, which we won't go into here). Think of the hundreds of people in a system called a "company," each of whom has slightly different interpretations of concepts like "competition," "performance," and "success." It is easy to see why there are complex problems within companies. Companies are systems that are designed to make things, sell them, and earn a profit. As people are added to the mix, along with their various cultures, different languages, individual values, and perceptions, creating, selling, and delivering products or services becomes complicated, to say the least.

Pictures and images used in a business context help to "contain" and capture the perceptions and the realities of people in organizations. When people share how they see and experience the business and someone draws it, a couple of things happen. Carlos Mota, a skilled facilitator and business consultant from Mexico, put it this way: "It's not like all the complexity and its components go away. When we capture people's stories and views visually, we get just enough of the detail to understand the dynamics and relationships, but not so much that it clutters our thinking. The visual images allow us to move above the complexity and see it [the system] as a total picture. When we can see it from a 'higher' place, we begin to understand the connections and dynamics between things." We begin to discern what is really a perception (for example, an assumption, a fixed opinion, or an impression that we have about something) and what is, for most, a reality (for example, profits diminishing, people leaving the organization, or competition taking market share).

Early in my professional career, I worked with an extraordinary domestic business in the United States. The leadership team was sophisticated, well educated, and experienced. The company had a strong philosophy of including people from all levels of its business in its strategic and long-range planning. It was in a growing industry that allowed it to create new products and test them with loyal customers. It seemed as if the stars were aligned for this business to grow and do great things. And yet, in the past 20 years, this firm has shrunk to one-quarter of its prior workforce and become a shadow of its former self. What happened?

There was a gap between perception and reality. This firm had had a very lucrative government contract that supported the base of the business. This allowed it to innovate and create new products for its other customers. However, government contracts expire, and you have to compete for them again. The company's leaders believed that the contract renewal was a "no-brainer." The company had all the right relationships, and while its product had recently lost patent protection, it dominated the industry. The leaders were convinced that there was no way the company would lose its government contract. But the leaders had a major blind spot. The main product they sold to and supported for the government was outdated. With the patent having expired and the contract being up, competitors saw an opportunity to design integrated and superior-performing alternatives with the specific intention of capturing the government contract. They did.

This is not the first time that something like this has happened to a business, but when the gap between the true reality and what is perceived as reality is as wide as the Grand Canyon, action needs to be taken. Organizations and teams that are facing this challenge can embrace relevant and traditional business processes that they know (like gap analysis, SWOT [strengths, weaknesses, opportunities, and threats] analysis, or environmental scan) to learn more about their gap. In the eyes of management, these are legitimate models and approaches to go through with our colleagues while the brain slows down, reflects, and uses the opportunity to, ideally, produce different results. Pictures are highly effective in any and all of these processes. When you conduct an analysis on a large piece of paper with colors and images, it may be messy, but employees and teams will see the gap and immediately begin thinking of ways to close it.

To get to the heart of the complexity as quickly as a system will let them, teams need to spend more time thinking about the questions they ask within one of the business models they use. Better-focused questions lead to better and more focused answers. For example, in a SWOT analysis, in looking at the "strengths" category, a team may ask, "What are we good at?" Would the analysis produce a different result if the team asked, "When our company is at its best, what are we doing? What are we saying? What are we producing?" Or, when the team considers "threats" in the SWOT process, could it ask, "What are the strengths of our competitors? How do we know this? How are we different?" to elicit a different intelligence that closes the gap between perception and reality effectively—and does it fast!

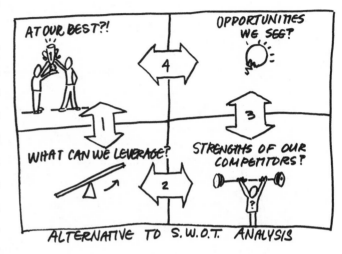

ALTERNATIVE TO S.W.O.T. ANALYSIS

Taking the time to think differently about the questions being asked in these processes will produce pictures that contain much of the complexity that a business faces, while quickly revealing barriers and assumptions. On the map, we can point to an assumption and go deeper, asking, "Why do we think that?" This is an effective way to peel away the layers of complexity so that we can understand what is urgent and what might be a distraction. Pictures and metaphors prompted by better and more relevant questions capture the complexity effectively in ways that allow teams to actually "see" it. They get above the situation to see critical relationships and to recognize blind spots and other elements that are holding them back from achieving success.

Capturing complexity is a way to think about the various influences within and on the business, such as operational and functional dynamics, competition, shrinking and changing markets, the organization's history, and important relationships for the team that may be tethered and relevant to new opportunities. These layers of complexity form the fabric of today's business. The "fibers" contain important information about our organizational DNA, our culture, the assumptions we have made, and how work gets done. If only a small group of people capture the complexities that they see and share the results with no one, then they are living within a construct that they have created. It may or may not represent a reality within the business. The only way to "fact-check" the complexities is to socialize the pictures, listen to what others see, and critique the output with others in the business based on the business approaches used. If you have a single page that provides a colorful visual representation, it takes teams and individuals little time to weigh in and discuss what they see relative to what is captured on the original map.

ORGANIZATIONAL DNA

CULTURE

SYSTEMS

STORIES

STRATEGY

Collaboration with others to understand what they see as complex actually contributes to shrinking the gap between the team's perception of itself in a given environment and the reality. This is not collaboration for the sake of building morale or to improve a score on an employee satisfaction survey. This is collaboration to collect *business intelligence* and gain clarity on key issues so that the business can seamlessly and effortlessly deliver. The good news is that collaboration, teamwork, and coordination are more common in business now than they have ever been. "When we began this process with one of our most important senior teams," a colleague in a major multinational corporation shared, "the picture they described and my own observations were completely different. It completely explained why we were having problems. They saw the gap, and so did I. We began to see how we could help each other by focusing on what was important in the business environment and what mattered for delivering."

John Chambers, the longstanding CEO of Cisco, reflected on this change in business in an interview with the *New York Times*. "I'm a command-and-control person," he explained. "I like being able to say turn right, and we truly have 67,000 people turn right. But that's the style of the past. Today's world requires a different leadership style—more collaboration and teamwork." Chambers has changed his leadership style to include and involve more people across the company because it makes good sense for his business.

In *That Used to Be Us*, Friedman and Mandlebaum share an interview with Ellen Kullman, DuPont's nineteenth CEO (from 2009). Kullman describes in detail what she looks for in every employee that the company hires, from senior vice president to line worker. "We want every employee to be present in the room. . . . Now you have to have people who can think and interact and collaborate. But to do that they have to be engaged and paying attention—*they have to be present*—so that they are additive, and not just taking up space. Whatever job you have in the company, you need to understand how your job adds value wherever you are [in the value chain]."

A direct result of a focus on collaboration and teamwork is that people expect and want to be involved in processes that can help them do their job better or add value. Including others in strategic business processes, such as developing the company's direction or prioritizing key initiatives for the year, supports Kullman's notion of being "present." Leaders can do their part by making what they

see (their perceptions) available to others to discuss, comment on, and add to through the use of visuals. Teams that work at all levels of the business see things that others don't. They have solutions or ideas that are pain- and cost-free, but they are rarely consulted about what they think. Engaging and involving employees at all levels to visually share what they see and how they experience work may hold the secret to what will move the business forward or reveal what is stalling its growth.

Capturing complexity also involves changing the collective stories that persist throughout the business. These stories lock in the way people view one another and even opportunities. The stories we tell reveal the distinct and firm patterns of behavior in the organization and are loaded with beliefs, assumptions, and expectations that have never been confirmed, denied, or validated by the leaders or by their teams. Complexity can be thought of as "the dynamic and intimate interactions [within a system] that happen in a given domain" (Carlos Mota), and stories are one of the most effective mechanisms for explaining and debunking the perceptions that lock people into seeing the world only one way.

The power of stories should not be underestimated. In Maggie Koerth-Baker's *New York Times Magazine* article "The Mind of a Flip-Flopper," Timothy Wilson, psychology professor at the University of Virginia and the author of *Redirect*, says, "Stories are more powerful than data . . . because they allow individuals to identify emotionally with ideas and people they might otherwise see as 'outsiders.'" Stories are memorable (this is why they travel like wildfire through organizations). They include both experiences and feelings. The aim is to move away from the stories that maintain and support the complexities of today, and move toward

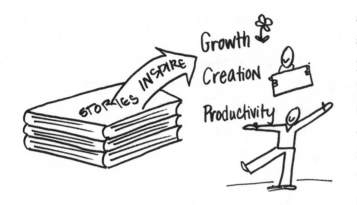

a new story that inspires growth, creation, and productivity. When complexities are adequately captured, we understand them. When we understand them, we can begin to let go of them as they hold us back from moving forward. It becomes easier to create a different story. New stories that are shared among the team are like picturing the outcome; they unleash the potential of a team and inspire the individual.

Storytelling in a business context needs to be authentic. Real stories reveal multiple insights into an organization's culture and systems. Visual images and metaphors can contribute to a story's authenticity and may emphasize key points if they are discussed with a strategic illustrator or graphic facilitator ahead of time so that the illustrator or facilitator can do this directly on the paper. The future of many businesses may depend on the stories that get told, who tells them, the barriers they reveal, and the trust they create. Stories build a sense of belonging and hope when individuals on a team hear and share their stories.

Drawing pictures of people's stories is a great way to capture complexities. Stories do not discriminate among people, places, feelings, and experiences. All of these complexities (and more) are there in any story. Because everything is included, stories lend

themselves to metaphors, visual templates, and images more read-
ily than a presentation or a report does.

Storytelling is often intimate and personal—one person is divulg-
ing an experience and feelings to another person that she works
with. Creating a productive and safe setting for the sharing of stories is part of the process of rebuilding trust and setting the stage
for alignment and movement forward. Providing opportunities for
each individual to share his story while others listen to him and then listening to their stories in
return is optimal. Humans love to tell and re-
tell our stories—it's how we explain certain
events that have happened to us (remember that we don't all see the same thing).
And we love to hear a good story—it helps
us understand the person who is telling the story, evokes empathy, and
builds new ties.

BUILDING NEW TIES

In the end, the individual stories that are shared become group
stories. As listeners, we experience what the storyteller experienced
and begin to see the workplace through her eyes. As team members describe what they have seen and heard, the listeners sense
their confusion, frustration, and lack of clarity. When these same
team members have someone drawing the world as they see it, they
begin to feel heard and listened to. Their "picture" is up in front of
the room, separate from the team itself, where everyone can see it.

SHARED
STORY

This is a validation of the perception contained in it. It is like an acknowledgment that whatever is there is real. At this point, with the stories and the complexity captured, the team can synthesize key issues that are common to the team or the business. Team members can quickly offer actions that need to be taken, volunteer to do them, and clarify the next steps. While this may feel like a circuitous route, the complexity captured on the map allows the team to move quickly into what needs to happen next.

The point of using stories in business is to close the perception-reality gap and to serve as a bridge to create a new story. The stories from the past shine a bright light on the patterns that have held the team back, and also on the assumptions and beliefs that have limited the team's abilities. Because the stories were shared with the team or the company on some level, they belong to everyone in the company. We remember these stories, we follow them, and, as individuals, *we grow in the direction of the stories that we tell.*

The visual image of the direction in which the company wants to grow is the key mechanism for *simplifying* what is seen and allowing a team to move on. The metaphor or image that gets captured at this point is something that almost everyone who was involved in the storytelling or who hears about the stories will give a nod to or acknowledge. "Yes," their verbal or nonverbal communication conveys, "I have this same feeling, the same experience."

The simpler the image, the better. You really don't need to know how to draw in order to create icons or images that get people's attention. Martha Lanaghen, CEO of the Sparrow Group and budding strategic illustrator/facilitator, shared a recent story about the quality of a flipchart she had created for a client. "They loved it! And they were so impressed that the simple stick figures and colors captured exactly what they were trying to clarify. Taking this step with my client really transformed how I feel about drawing in the context of business. I had always been worried about the drawings being 'pretty.' After seeing how they [my clients] reacted to my rudimentary and crude images, I have the courage to draw more, and more often." Having the courage to use images is 75 percent of the challenge in capturing complexities. Images do so much more than words.

The icons and images that get used at this point frequently reflect a journey, such as a ship, a road, a car, a rocket, or a climb up a mountain. Individuals talk about their professional experiences as if they are on some kind of trip: "I was really stuck," or "Gosh, I feel like I can really move on now. Where should we go?" The metaphor is anchored in the experience and feeling of moving, making it easy to "read" the map or tell the story behind it. The great thing about "journey" metaphors is that they are multicultural. Everyone left home at some point in time, and because of this universal experience, both team members and those outside the team will look at the map and see where they "fit in" psychologically.

Whatever metaphor the team or business settles on, it provides the clarity and the energy that the team needs to both be in the moment and let go of the past at the same time. This may seem contradictory, but people who release themselves from being stuck actually have the energy to move on. By articulating their feelings and the situation in a metaphor—a great picture—the team members see everything that has contributed to the complexity and, individually and collectively, can let go of what was holding them back and get on to the future.

Capturing complexity by using images, metaphors, and stories is extraordinarily memorable. It is the result of deep listening—of people really hearing what is being said and felt at new levels. These stories also represent a level of vulnerability that is not typically seen in a business environment. "I remember my boss looking so lonely when he was telling us how he felt, what his experience with us was like," a participant in a strategy session recalled. "I wanted to tell him

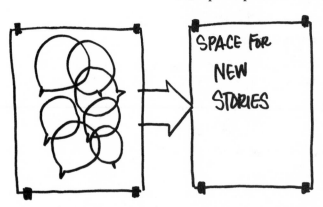

that we were here for him. He did not have to go through all that alone." This "human touch," authentically shared and captured, provides a catalyst for change. The collective stories, captured and contained in a map, create the space for new stories to emerge.

Once pictured, complexity can be affirmed and validated by the group, signifying that, "Yes, this happened, and we are moving on." The map and its pictures are a tangible extension of the history, institutional memory, knowledge, and feelings within the business. People and their stories are heard, some of them for the first time. The map represents the commonality of perspectives and feelings, the trust and the camaraderie that the team can use going forward to tackle a new and bright future.

To capture complexity successfully, remember the following:

1. Bridge the perception-reality gap with the right questions, in the right order parallel to business strategy. Do this with pictures!

2. Share the picture of the gap and possible answers with your team or with as large a group as possible so that people can see how the collective thinking is perceived and seen by others.

3. Use storytelling and pictures to disrupt your linear way of thinking about the complexities within an organization. This way of working helps you to picture people, systems, and structures in new ways. People let go of the past and are ready to think about the future.

4. Simplify. Remember that everyone can fit into a picture, and the simpler it is, the better.

5. Validate. The emerging images belong to the group. Simple icons create consensus and agreement on key issues and actions to be taken going forward.

CREATE
POSSIBILITIES

ACT THREE: CREATE POSSIBILITIES

In the story, after Sean met with the senior team, the next steps were fairly straightforward. They had a plan, and they knew what actions they needed to take in the next few months with one goal: to cut through the inertia that had settled into the organization. The team reflected on organizational complexity in new ways, captured it in one place, and began to see what might be possible. There was new energy in the group—remember that Sean commented that morale had improved. The pictures created in the senior team meeting provided an easy way for people to focus on what was important. However, the first picture of their strategy took the team and the division only so far.

When the whole division met together and effectively "decluttered" their workspace, freeing them from the perceptions, stories, and myths that bound them to their current state of performance, the next steps for the division became clear. Together, they captured complexity, synthesized key activities, and moved forward with new interest and energy. The people in the division continued to use the tangible map as a way to remind them of their focus. As they executed their plan, they created a whole new idea of themselves. With new energy and a focus on the hard tasks that lay ahead, they were able to turn the business around. They were able to do all this in one day.

As illustrated in this story, a business strategy developed with pictures is a strategic mechanism for energizing, exciting, aligning, and focusing a team. The pictures created serve as a lighting rod for the creation of new ideas, inspiration, and motivation. This approach works, in part, because it taps into things that motivate people intrinsically. "We believe that intrinsic motivation must be present if people are to do their best," James Kouzes and Barry Posner explain in *The Leadership Challenge.* "We believe that what *is* rewarding gets done. . . . [We need to] tap into people's hearts and minds, not merely their hands and wallets." Picturing the outcome and capturing complexity allows for a focus on what *is* rewarding for the members of a team, division, or business relative to the business. Leaders and managers can look at the maps and clearly see and remember what people talked about that created a certain buzz and excitement in the room. The part of the map that represents intrinsic motivation can be used when executing the business strategy. Kouzes and Posner remind us that "the key to intrinsic motivation is getting involved in something that requires us to look at a situation in new ways." New ways to look at a situation inevitably create possibilities for the business.

A great example of a process in which intrinsic motivation came together through the use of a pictured strategy is a large hospital system located in Denver, Colorado. We were working with a group of doctors in one of the hospital's divisions to create a vision of the doctors' work and their contribution to the hospital system where they worked. Lois Todd, senior partner at Alchemy, described the process: "It's like it almost happened in a flash. The doctors suddenly saw how they fit into the whole business and the work of the hospital. Right in that moment, they began talking about their work and the division in a completely new way. It was clear through their language and facial/body expressions, something had changed. The insight they all arrived at had a profound impact on the group. The doctors finally understood they were part of something. They could see and feel the contributions they were making, and they were connected to and motivated by their collective commitment to the field of medicine and people's health. This was a huge motivator." It was not enough that the doctors had created a vision. The picture they had created contained the possibility of new relationships among themselves, the other departments, and the whole business. When they "saw" it, they were excited to be part of something that was beyond their individual work or their department.

As people look at a business visual that has been created, they intuitively tap into the connections that they see. They become aware of what they are doing now and connect it to what could potentially happen later. Our intrinsic motivator pushes us to populate the picture with the individual contributions that we want to make, defining how we fit into the picture. Our brains and the group's ideas do not wait for a boss or a senior manager to tell them what to do. Teams are motivated by the pictures they see, and they create their role, imagining how they are going to contribute. One client recently said about an action plan done for his team, "It was amazing the energy, focus, and attention people had coming out of our meeting. In four hours we were able to create something that everyone bought into, something that provided short- and mid-term focus and a way for people to engage. It was like throwing fuel on a fire." It can be like fuel to energize, catalyze, and motivate people to deliver because they have direction and focus, and they were a part of setting the course of action.

What is it about the work of linking business strategy and pictures that cuts through the typical complexity and bureaucracy of business and leads to a level of clarity and motivation? Pictures cut through the hierarchical, structural world of the left brain. Because pictures can mean many things to many people, all definitions, words, and interpretations are included. This flattens assumptions, beliefs, and perceptions, making all things equal. Regardless of who contributed what to a map, everyone's comments and images count; everything matters. As a result, when employees create a business strategy in pictures, they seamlessly talk about how they see new ways of working together as they look at the whole picture. They may parcel out pieces because it makes sense for one group to do something or for one activity to go first, but they do this because it makes sense within the big picture, not because someone told them to do it.

In one example, teams that worked with mounds of data and analytics within a business were able to make new connections among themselves, their work, the indicators they track in spreadsheets, and activity in other departments. At a recent conference of leaders from around the globe, one participant from Asia pointed out something on a map and said, "Before this conference, I did not really see how the five goals of our department were connected. The way you drew it here," he pointed, "the connections are starting to make sense to me. Can I take a picture? I want to e-mail this to my team."

In a left-brain linear world, it is not always easy to pick out the connections or possible ties to other work flow, people, and pro-

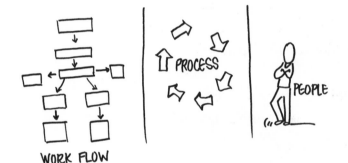

WORK FLOW

cesses. In the case of business and strategy, our right brain picks up where the picture leaves off and imagines, connects, and creates ideas, solutions, and new ways of working. These insights can be added, changed, mapped, and discussed by the group, creating a deeper understanding among the team members about the direction, focus, and priorities they want to work toward. In the same way that the pictures help the brain cut through bureaucracy, teams and those who are using the pictures as part of their strategic process can also cut through organizational malaise and clarify what's important, why, and what it will take to make it possible.

One of the things that prevents teams and individuals from seeing and creating possibilities is fear—fear of failure, fear of exclusion, and fear of not fitting in. As discussed earlier, fear is a powerful toxin within organizations that can destabilize great cultures and ruin organizational performance. Fear can be a hard thing to combat in an organization because it is an individual condition that manifests itself in a group setting. Pictures in business help to alleviate people's fear of failure and exclusion. These pictures provide a path and a direction forward that the team has agreed to. Everyone is included in the image. The strategy and execution cannot get done without every person being involved.

This story tells it best.

Elizabeth Groginsky, a well-known leader in the field of early childhood education, was part of the leadership team of a large collaborative organization just outside the city of Denver that supports young people in excelling in their community regardless of their background or economic circumstances (Adams County Youth Initiative, http://www.acyi.org).

> We had one day to get 35 people on the same page and aligned to take the program to the next level. Our partners and programs expanded, and we needed to factor more people, programs, and services into our core work. Many of the people in the room were meeting each other for the first time: police officers from eight different jurisdictions, a group of local citizens, childcare providers, educators from five school districts, and county employees. This new group needed to clarify and visualize who we were with new partners, who we serve, what kind of support we would provide, and why we would provide

that kind of support. We needed to do this in a way that allowed for everyone's input, while also providing focus, clarity, and direction.

As you might imagine, the police in the room were skeptical of this type of process. Individually, we were not comfortable with their presence simply because we did not know them or how to work collaboratively with them. For a collaboration to happen, we needed their buy-in, support, and commitment. Having someone else guiding the conversation and capturing it visually allowed the rest of us to relax and focus on listening to and getting to know one another. We were able to talk about what mattered to us from our positions in the community and as residents. We built new relationships with one another because we all spoke about what mattered to us. At the beginning of the day, no one believed that we could accomplish what we set out to do. But we did! We achieved our goal and then some. The picture showed it. By the end of the day, there was a shared sense of accomplishment and pride. This group used the map at every meeting for the next year. It went everywhere with us. We used it to validate, explain, review, and support our work.

The individuals in the group were able to let go of their fears by focusing on what everyone in the group cared about. They prioritized their vision and their mission based on the contributions of the stakeholders around the table. They were able to see a collective commitment emerge through pictures, words, and color. The large-scale map served as an important reminder that they were in the collaboration because they wanted to be there together, and all perspectives and all points of view within the organization were represented and featured in the visual.

Lisa Bardwell, CEO and president of the national nonprofit organization Earth Force (www.earthforce.org), shared part of her story in creating a business strategy visually portrayed:

> We have always been a hard organization to understand. And, an even harder organization to explain to others. We were in the process of changing our already complicated business model and going through the process of designing and building a one-page visual that explained the new way our organization would work. It was the perfect way for our staff and partners to actually see where they fit into the new "picture" of the organization and how the different parts of the system work together to support young people in communities all over the world. Part of the story that is visualized is literal. There are places on the map where the viewer sees young people doing what we do with them in our communities. And part of our story is metaphorical. When leaders in other communities are interested in working with us, this picture shows them what the possibility of working in partnership with us

can be. They see themselves, their young people, parents, community members and businesses in the map. Our visual is both a picture of our work and a vision of how we want the world to be. When I show investors and funders our picture, they get it! They are immediately engaged, and they want to know how to get involved—not why.

Both of these stories highlight how inclusive pictures can be used to mitigate the damage that penetrates an organization when fear of the unknown enters our brains and the organizational psyche. John Hunt, in his book *The Art of the Idea*, reflects on fear in this way: "Usually . . . fear is rooted in the need for the change to present itself in a neat, orderly fashion. We want the future to be revealed in sequential bite-size chunks that are easily digestible. Unfortunately, the world doesn't operate that way and pretending it does creates the perfect killing field for ideas." Pictures embedded in a business strategy will help new ideas and possibilities flourish while easing our individual and collective fear concerning everything that a change implies.

In the same way that they help ease our fears of failure and exclusion, pictures break down language barriers. We have all experienced conversations in which we thought that what we had communicated was clear, but it turned out that the person meant something completely different. Miscommunication can happen even with people who speak the same language, and it can have unfortunate and unintended consequences. The reason words and language fail us is that we don't use the right words to say something, our message is taken out of context, or we did not think through what we would say before we said it. This can often hurt people's feelings, contribute to an environment of distrust, and absolutely break down teams and their collective work.

When thoughtfully used images are combined with words in an appropriate context, the combination can have a lasting, profound, and powerful effect on teams and businesses. If you recall, in Sean's story, Cheryl shared an image of an action plan with him on her phone. I borrowed that image from an action planning map I created in 2004. The employees agreed on a tree as their organizational and cultural metaphor. The roots provided the resources that allowed the rest of the organizing to sustain itself. The "fruit" and "leaves" represented the innovative relationships, products, and opportunities created. The people in finance, operations, human resources,

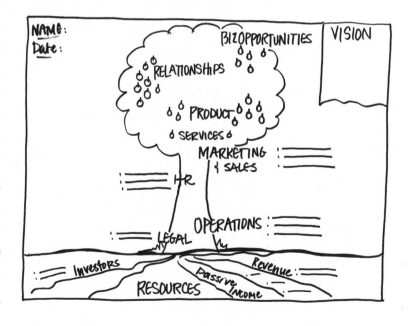

marketing, and sales saw themselves as unique parts of the tree. Together, they agreed on business targets and goals to be achieved in the context of a living and growing symbol. This planning experience broke down several functional barriers, and the teams were able to work more closely with one another going forward. They were able to do this because they had a common "language" in the metaphor of the tree. They recognized what would happen to the tree without the others' input and support. Lisa Bardwell from Earth Force shared this same sentiment. "Our strategy map has built a whole new language for us in the organization. We emphasize certain parts of the map with different audiences, and the language we use reinforces the images and metaphors they see. It's a self-supporting way of embedding new ideas with partners and funders using a shared language that is unique to our organization."

In multicultural business environments, pictures as metaphors can quickly help to orient people from different countries who speak different languages and focus them around key activities and priorities. Think about the images used on our smartphones to indicate texting, e-mail, and contacts. Each of these communicates an activity simply, effectively, and universally. Simple pictures used in business strategy will create the same connections for people who come from different parts of the world but live inside the same organizational culture. They can be useful institutional "anchors" that provide direction and action in ways that a corporate newsletter or memo cannot. They also free up employees to think about their

work and focus on it rather than trying to interpret what is really being said in a written or even an oral format.

Pictures, metaphor, and color are important components that help unleash people's ideas when they are exploring and creating possibilities for a business. I have not yet been with a client who has not asked about the ROI (return on investment) on any engagement where visuals are used. Face it, creating possibilities and executing them are a cost to the business. It takes time, expertise, and resources to implement whatever possibility gets identified as something that will happen. If a business is going to invest in creating and implementing a bunch of possibilities, will this deliver more value (money, reputation, resources, or savings) to the business?

The concept of delivering ROI with a business strategy that is in the form of pictures is an important thing to explore. Let's first start by looking at strategy in our businesses today. Strategic planning processes are usually more events than an integral part of how we work every day. Because strategy and execution (along with management and delivering results) are hard to do simultaneously, we break the two activities apart. We go so far as to hold strategy sessions over a couple of days at an outside location. This physically, emotionally, and psychologically separates strategic activity from the operational

or executing activity. Does this approach deliver a "bang" for the dollars spent?

In some ways, yes. The operational, execution side of our work lives is cluttered and full of distraction. Physical space at the office is at a premium, and virtual space is taken up with social media, e-mail, conference calls, and other day-to-day interruptions. When we go away from the office to discuss it, strategic activity is given a focus, and this sends a signal of its level of importance to the business. Going away also has benefits. A different nonoffice environment provides the physical space for us to explore possibilities and frees us up to experiment with new ways of planning and working. It is fun, it builds morale and team spirit, and it can deliver long-range benefits and actions that make the investment of time and resources worthwhile.

The downsides to off-site events are costs, lack of frequency (once a year at best), and the fact that not everyone can make it. While the face time and human interaction that these events create are invaluable, can teams get some of these same benefits by doing other things more regularly? The reality that strategy and planning are not part of everyday business life is a problem. Ideally, companies live and execute their strategy every day. Strategy becomes even further removed when it is taken out of the business. It typically stays outside the business, becoming an isolated event at which a lot is discussed, but only a little gets done.

As a leader, I have seen the direct benefits of picturing the outcome, capturing complexities, and creating possibilities with teams on a weekly or monthly basis. These principles can also build morale, team spirit, and fun around the work that people do every day. In on-site events, the principles and accompanying visuals become part of the lifeblood of the culture in which they are practiced and put into place. Pictures and visual images used in meetings, presentations, planning, product roll-out sessions, and financial target setting are then visual bridges between what you are thinking and planning and what you are doing. The pictures are powerful and can broadly communicate important concepts across languages in the same way they are described in this book. Teams can easily track performance, they can correct their course, or they can evaluate their success in carrying out a strategy that is given on one page and portrayed visually, whether they are in the office or at a warehouse. Teams are engaged and in a position to anticipate and respond to opportunities when they arise, not wait until an annual off-site meeting.

The visual map that you create is a deliverable that guides a team internally and guides its activities externally. It is easy to carry with you. There have not been many strategic planning processes or business planning sessions that I have attended where I can print out a copy of the plan and send it to my smartphone or take it with me. Just like a city map or a road map, this map becomes the visual guide for the team members, whether they are new to the organization or embedded in the team that actually created the plan. The visual serves as a reference point and reminds the team of its direction, providing focus when things are confusing or overwhelming. The pictures allow managers and leaders to ease up on their top-down management approach and use the visual to discuss progress, changes, and results with the teams that they manage. The large map of pictures gets used; it tracks activities and supports teams to achieve their success and business leaders to deliver results. This is great ROI on a fast-paced, simple, and inexpensive approach to planning, strategy, and execution.

While picturing a business strategy in the moment is a real thrill, the deeper gratification and the ultimate return on investment take place when a person looks at the map one, two, or even six months later. The individual and the team recall what it took to get to the final outcome, and how they felt before, during, and after the process. Someone on the team may even point to specific things that were said, recall who agreed to them, and remember who commented on what. When people in an organization use the picture to explain to a customer or a new employee who they are, what they do, why they do it, and what they intend to accomplish, these customers and employees are immediately visually and emotionally engaged. New employees can see themselves and where they fit in. Customers are thrilled that the business thought enough about them to put them in a segment of the map. Business leaders and others can easily engage in the story behind the map. Those individuals who are brand new to the map and the process will ask clarifying questions, enquire about the process, and be excited to see "what's next." The picture is pleasing to them psychologically. It's intellectually and "left-brain" stimulating because it is about direction and performance, and because they see where they fit.

"The map gives me a kind of emotional confidence. Everything I need to know or think about will be evoked through the picture. This is my talking point and collateral. I don't need anything else," commented Lisa Bardwell of Earth Force.

"Before every engagement with a client or organization, I sit down and draw a one-page visual summary of what I see. This is not a tool or a methodology for me," says Carlos Mota from Mexico. "It's a way of seeing. A way to give meaning to what I see about their [my client's] business and situation. It's a way to comprehend a client's situation and see it from multiple angles and dimensions."

It's remarkable. On one page, an individual and her team can create a picture that captures the complexity of their work and their business while increasing clarity and gaining consensus about things that can be dealt with tomorrow. In one day, teams are able to create the space they need in order to take two or three new ideas forward and work toward something new. The map builds a new language for teams in the business; they can make the map a part of their culture, and it provides them with a different way to focus and interact with their peers and colleagues. As teams get more accustomed to working with their maps and other visuals that they create, the quality of the conversations will improve. The team will spend its resources on strategizing, delivering against that strategy, and creating new business opportunities rather than trying to figure out where it is going and how that decision got made. Pictures deliver in ways that other things cannot.

A final note about creating possibilities. Humans are born to create. In *The Heart of Leadership*, author Sabina Spencer shares, "Much of our sense of self-worth comes from our ability to be generative—it is why we are here. Creation is our birthright, and if we don't express our passion we remain unfulfilled." When the opportunity, need, or desire arises, humans rise to the challenge of creating something. Whether it is planting seeds and waiting for them to grow, building a tree house, creating a beautiful and sleek smartphone, constructing a massive dam to hold back water, or getting a man to the moon and home again, our deepest shared desire is to create something. This desire does not leave us when we go to work. It lies there, waiting for us to create something of value.

In business, we know stories of companies that have taken advantage of a creative offshoot with great success. DuPont has products that are derived from inferior-quality Corian and Tyvek. 3M waited almost five years before it entertained the thought of commercializing an adhesive error that we know today as Post-its. People within these companies spent time creating a product from a mistake. This only scratches the surface of tapping into this human desire to create. There are many stories about businesses that give their employees a day a month to work on whatever they want to as long as they share their work with the company. Some of these stories feature employees who are not engineers and do not specialize in creative work with the company. When they are given the space to explore and see what can be fixed, they find ways to save money, streamline a process, or create value through a system or a structural change. People are intrinsically motivated, but some of these creative results are also rewarded.

In this day and age of lean and tight budgets, the idea of paying people to work on something other than their job seems risky, untraditional, and for some "other business"—not yours. While we have heard or read about the benefits of such activities (such as new patents, new products, and simple ideas to save money), we remain skeptical that such a practice will deliver anything other than people abusing the system and taking full advantage of the opportunity for "not working." However, while abuses of such a system probably do occur, there is something bigger at play here.

We spoke about intrinsic motivation earlier in this section. The human desire to create is deeply linked to the things that intrinsically motivate us. People are given freedom when businesses take a risk and provide the conditions that allow their employees to create in the context of their work and for the company. When the right conditions are provided to support creativity, productivity, and ingenuity, people make contributions that are beyond themselves and their work. They do it happily and willingly.

As I have studied groups of people who are very successful at what they do (firefighters, athletes, musicians, artists, economists, futurists, and philosophers), they have several elements in common. One of these is that they find or create the optimal conditions for success. Optimal conditions can be defined as having the right equipment, resources, lighting, sound, space, coaching, and support. This is how they win, perform a difficult piece of music, or save someone's life in a fire. These individuals and teams practice. They place themselves in all kinds of scenarios to ensure that they can perform under any conditions and still achieve their goal.

For example, in the 2012 Olympics, Ryan Lochte used a new training program to gain the strength, endurance, and stamina required for him to break world records in swimming and beat his fellow swimmer, Michael Phelps. It worked. In the *Art of Possibility*, conductor Benjamin Zander talks about giving each of his students an A at the beginning of the semester so that the pressure to get an A is removed and his pupils can focus on their music. Thus, even before they have worked with him, Zander creates the conditions for his students to succeed. Bending the way people think about themselves, their performance, and their opportunity is also part of creating possibilities. Creating the conditions enables the possibilities to be realized—producing winning results.

How often do we consciously create the conditions required to succeed in business? "Well, business is different," we might think. "What you are talking about requires time, forethought, and some planning. And the business landscape changes all the time. Can we afford to change and take a risk with some of the ways we work? Everything is running just fine now. How could this possibly lead to profitability?"

Think back to a time in your career when you accomplished a goal that you or your team had set out to achieve. What conditions were present that enabled your success? Perhaps you were given a lighter workload and extra space to focus on the project. Perhaps you had leadership support and others who were there to help if needed. You may have felt as if you had been invited to do or create something that you were uniquely qualified and able to do. You stepped into whatever opportunity presented itself and achieved success.

When there is a clear picture of the outcome, complexity has been sidelined, and the conditions for success have been created (such as support, financial or people resources, or coaching from a colleague or peer), watch out! This type of alignment and energy drives the deep human desire to achieve, to contribute, and to share. It creates a sense of "newness" or "adventure." As the possibilities are captured visually and the individual or the team takes off in the creating process, that individual or team is armed with the clarity, focus, and direction that the pictured business strategy provides.

In summary, to successfully enable creating possibilities, remember that:

- Business strategy developed in pictures connects with what motivates people intrinsically and produces energy, excitement, alignment, and focus.

- Pictures allow the right brain to cut in front of the left-brain way of organizing information. New connections, ideas, and solutions emerge because pictures provide a different way of looking at the world.

- Pictures help temper our fear of isolation; we feel what it means to belong when we are part of creating a shared picture.

- Visuals break down language barriers. This works in global multinational businesses and in small local enterprises. What a difference it makes when we all speak the same language.

- Business strategy presented in pictures delivers a new and different ROI for the business. It's fast-paced and energizing. It's a single-page tangible object that people can take with them in hard or soft copy and use. It's always in their "back pocket."

- Pictures tap into the desire of all humans to create. These pictures help create the conditions for success.

CHAPTER 5

FROM

__Alignment__

to acceleration

The three principles (picture the outcome, capture complexity, and create possibilities) provide business leaders and managers with a simple set of ideas that they can use in a variety of business situations every day and all the time. We have explored pairing these activities with a picture so that shared stories and plans can emerge and be seen within organizations. We have also discussed why sharing, comparing, and conversing about these pictures with many people on (and outside of) the team is important. A consistent shared story is a form of collective intelligence that is hard to capture in words alone. The images provide the backdrop of energy, commitment, and engagement that words alone do not capture.

The previous chapter described the benefits that result when the three principles—picture the outcome, capture complexity, and create possibilities—are used independent of one another. There are benefits gained, and teams are able to move on to work that delivers value.

When the three principles are used in tandem and linked together, however, ideas, strategies, and energy quickly converge to create the conditions for success.

There is a large-scale policy initiative at the Meridian Institute (www.merid.org) called AGree: transforming food and agriculture policy (www.foodandagpolicy.org). The aim of AGree is to address the most important challenges the world faces in the next 15 to 20 years in the areas of food and agriculture. With support from nine foundations, AGree is boldly examining tough issues like the paradox of obesity and extreme hunger, consciously improving the environment at the same time that we sustain (and increase) the production and harvesting of food, workforce challenges ranging from immigration to attracting young people into food and agricultural careers, and considering options that will feed the world between now and 2030. AGree involves a diverse and experienced group of stakeholders who have set the vision, the direction, and the subsequent actions of this effort.

The issues and challenges that AGree is committed to exploring and changing through partnerships, policy, and legislation touch every human in some way. The reality is that every person has to eat. How we get our food, how much it costs, and the choices we make concerning it are things that are a part of every person's daily life, young or old. Because these issues touch every person, systems have been created to manage every aspect of the food "supply chain." Part of the reason AGree was created is that the systems and silos that exist within the current system were not designed with the challenges of the twenty-first century in mind. Globalization, changes in weather, distribution and storage costs, disease, crop loss, the renewed interest in what people eat and where it comes from, chemicals, health issues—the list goes on and challenges the system at every turn. This eight-year-old program is complex and diverse. And large-scale maps and pictures have been used from the very beginning to picture a set of possible outcomes within an integrated and harmonized system—to make meaning of the complexity, to catalyze conversations among different stakeholder groups, and to help decision makers "see" the possibilities in some of the proposed policy and program changes.

Todd Barker, senior partner and lead facilitator with AGree, summed it up this way: "It's not so much about the quality of the drawing. That's really secondary. What is more important is the interaction the pictures create. The pictures allow people to talk with each other about what they see and how they see it. It also provides a way for people to interact with their own ideas. When I see someone walk up to the map, I can visibly see that person wrestling with the complexity, the relationship between ideas and the challenges. These maps give meaning and structure to the issues we are dealing with that just cannot happen in words. Even if we tried to write it, we would miss the connections that are vital to making a change."

AGree is employing every principle and using many of the business models discussed. It has created the right conditions to have this conversation, and the timing for considering and proposing new possibilities for the system is also right. It has involved many people in picturing the outcome, capturing complexity, and creating possibilities through the new connections, relationships, and information that these people see and share. By combining activities from the three principles with pictures, a convergence of belief, opportunity, energy, and the desire for action is created. I call this *conditional convergence*—the right conditions create a convergence of ideas, beliefs, and values that produce alignment and acceleration.

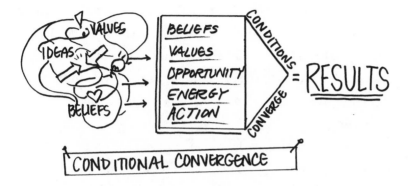

Peter Senge and his team of writers in *The Dance of Change* put it best: "Aligning people to a shared set of aspirations (vision, purpose, values and guiding principles) can be a lot of work. Why put in the effort? Because the results are worth it. If people are going to the same place, share the same values, and work within the same guiding principles, these shared aspirations can take the place of other means of ensuring coordination and alignment, such as top-down supervision and rules. . . . Aligned aspirations are also the reference point that give you constant orientation and focus, and allow you to redesign the airplane as you are flying it."

Alignment is the key. Picturing the outcome, capturing complexity, and creating possibilities are essential for conditional convergence. When these principles are used together with pictures and business strategy, the combination serves as a platform for harnessing and focusing energy, building and maintaining momentum, and rapidly closing the distance between where you are and where you want to be, transforming the way business decisions are made and getting work done. Alignment provides the fuel needed to achieve the business outcomes that a person and his team envision. Everyone has to be on the same page, moving in the same direction with a feeling and sense of agreement concerning the movement.

An easy and elegant definition of *alignment* for business can be borrowed from other disciplines, including biology, education, astronomy, anatomy, geology, typography, and transportation. Alignment is best defined as "physical construction of systems and relationships in an arrangement that makes or supports functionality and movement." When we connect the three principles, we create an integrated structure that allows for the preservation of the work you have done and enables people to see the picture in a complete way. When we connect the visual images created along the way, it allows for collective understanding of the direction; ideas are included, and actions are visualized.

The use of the triangle as a symbol or icon of this integrated approach is deliberate. Triangles fill our early childhood memories in various ways.

We find simple comfort in the stick figure and the home. We know how to draw them. A triangle is also a mathematical symbol for change (delta)—the distance or gap between a set of variables. An equilateral triangle is one of the most stable of geometric shapes: the equal angles support the equal sides of the triangle. In the work of the first business innovators, the ancient alchemists, the triangle represented the ability to get closer to our truest aspirations—that which leads us closer to the divine.

As we examine the interrelationship between the three principles and the use of pictures, several things emerge. First, and perhaps most important, the true realization of the business strategy pictured is not possible if only *one* of the principles is present. Let's think about this. If you have visualized an outcome, but you are still mired in complexities and cannot see important connections, how will you know what to focus on first to achieve the outcome that you envision? Or if you have created a whole list of possibilities and even the space to pursue them, but you don't have a clear idea of why you are doing this or what it may lead to, how effective or relevant will those possibilities be when they are realized? Furthermore, if you have captured all the complexities in such a way that everyone can see them, but you have not explored what might be possible within the complexities themselves, what can you expect as the outcome? Like a lopsided three-legged stool, when one leg is missing, the stool is ineffective. It does not have the stability that it has when all three legs (the principles) are present.

When all the principles work together, they create a shared picture that is grounded in reality and that includes individual and collective aspirations. This helps to build the alignment and validation for a way to move forward that makes sense, that people can see, and that has energy behind it. A great example of this involved a technology firm based in Colorado. The CEO knew that he needed a way to get people on the same page about the business. Being in the technology field meant that the landscape the firm works in changes rapidly. The CEO was looking at the complexity of the business, the

potential of his people and his organization, and what he wanted to accomplish. He knew about some of the strongly held opinions among the staff members about how the products and services the company offered needed to change. "I knew we needed a simple way to look at things," he explains. "It was my daughter who inspired the need for a picture. She was trained in graphic recording and uses it at her school. I thought to myself, I wonder if we could do this in a picture." After several conversations with his team, an off-site meeting, developing a strategic plan, and some work on the right image that would carry the CEO and the team's story, we came up with a picture that shows business activity aligned with goals, people and their roles defined through the use of images, and the results that they have agreed to and expect. All the principles were at work at different times during the process. We did not have a completely "balanced" approach or strategy until right at the end, when the picture actually pulled everything together.

The CEO commented on the process and the final pictured strategy. "We came together around a picture that says what we want to be, how we want to be it, and why. This map serves as our guide and a way to talk about and measure our business. It has been a rallying cry of sorts and a way to explain and discuss a unique and outstanding company culture."

Second, alignment in simple terms can also be thought of as an agreement. A group of people who agree to go forward have a focus and a shared understanding of how work will get done and why. They acknowledge that their goal will take hard work, but they are committed to it through their shared sense of purpose and their focus on the outcome. They also feel emotionally attached to the agreement—like a promise, it goes beyond compliance and is at the heart of personal and professional commitment.

This type of alignment is such a simple idea, and yet it is hard to achieve and sustain. When we have it, we have buy-in, commitment, energy, and focus. When we don't have it, we have arguments, apathy, frustration, isolation, and lack of productivity. Teams and divisions in organizations move back and forth between having alignment and not having it—it's elusive and fluid. The images and pictures that are created during a visual strategy process are key to bringing people back into alignment. The images remind individuals of their agreement and their commitment to the outcome. When we don't have alignment, it can be isolating and cold. The use of images, metaphors, and color takes us out of the isolated feelings and helps us converse with our peers about the barriers we face. The pictures can help us get at the heart of the issues, even if

the challenge and struggle required are not visualized. The picture contains information that we have shared and that has roots in our own collective thinking. The process and the images help to support the "agreements" that we make with one another.

If the team or business forgets to bring something important to the surface, it usually shows up after people are aligned and working hard toward their outcome. Just because the team members did not see an obstacle or a problem does not mean that they have failed. It does mean that the picture and the processes used to create the map did not go far enough to unearth the critical things that stand in the way. Taking the picture further by thinking about the details and conditions described from multiple angles and including the perspective of others outside the team can increase the team members' commitment to one another while producing even greater alignment with the final outcome or goal.

As mentioned at the beginning of this book, we desperately need new ways to build the kind of agreements and alignment we need if we are to succeed in a competitive world. One of the founders of the World Café and coauthor of *The World Café Book: Shaping Our Futures Through Conversations That Matter*, Juanita Brown, put it this way: "Visual language helps people build on each other's ideas. Everyone has a chance to draw what they see and consult and talk with others on what they have drawn. They can understand how they see each other. With the disintegration of the once stable and enormous institutions that we trusted, we need new, less hierarchical ways to connect with one another. In the face of this (social, economic, and environmental) breakdown, visual language, the art of harvesting and sharing collective wisdom around critical issues, provides new ways to work together and develop viable paths forward."

The visual language used and described by Brown promotes the type of agreement and alignment needed. We can share what people think and understand why they think or believe the things they do because we can see them through the pictures that they draw or that we draw together. These images allow us to talk about ideas and concerns in ways we never could before.

In 2002, Janet Ross, the executive director and founder of the Four Corners School of Outdoor Education (www.fourcorners school.org), asked for some help with an important and potentially controversial community project. Her business is based in Monticello, Utah, a small town in the southern part of the state, located near the intersection of four states: Arizona, Colorado, New Mexico, and Utah. Her program served teachers, students, and adults from the area and around the United States by providing innovative education programs using the outstanding outdoors and natural resources in the region as the classroom. The classroom extends from watersheds to mountain peaks, from desert to canyons.

The Economic Development Committee of the city approached Janet about building a hands-on science center as a way to draw more tourists to the area and help boost the tax base and local businesses. This was an extraordinary invitation in many respects, but to be direct, the majority of the city and the county's population is Mormon. My colleague was not. Given the numbers of Mormons in the county, they run many of the basic services in the area, own many local businesses, and serve as local and county government officials. Several of the members of the Economic Development Committee had a vision of a science center as a new economic driver in their community. Very few of them knew how to build such a center, but they knew that if they enlisted someone in the community who knew how to make this happen, they could create something unique and special.

Monticello is in one of the poorest counties in the United States. It is near the Navajo Reservation and in the heart of some of the most beautiful national parks, forests, and public land in the United States. In this area, 8 percent of the land is privately owned, 25 percent is tribal, and 67 percent is public land. The county is hard-pressed to provide even the most basic services, since there are not enough people who own property and pay taxes to support the community's basic needs.

Through a series of publicly held meetings, convenings, and articles in the local paper, support for the idea built slowly. Funds were raised from the Economic Development Administration (EDA) to conduct market feasibility studies and write a business plan for the idea. Throughout the entire process, the three principles—picturing the outcome, containing complexity, and creating possibilities—were employed. A community leadership team continued to share its vision with members of the community. They modified and added to the overall picture of what people saw, including what they thought was possible. The complexities of bringing such an enterprise to a small town were openly discussed. Locals were concerned about how many people from outside the area the facility would attract, and how to balance that with serving local students and families. The community openly discussed what content would be taught at the center and why.

It appeared that the community of Monticello was aligned with moving forward with a new learning facility and taking a chance on what that facility would bring in terms of new revenues and possibilities. I recall a focus group meeting that was the tipping point for the project. The project team met with a group of women leaders from the community one afternoon. The team had developed a visual as a simple way to engage in conversation with other stakeholder groups. It used the same visual with all focus groups so that information and input were asked for and captured in the same way across all groups. After the introduction, a member of the team invited the women to talk about opportunities they saw and concerns they had about the project. The response was silence—icy at best. In spite of the cakes and hospitality, the room felt hostile. After about 15 minutes in this environment, I stepped back quietly to let silence seep into the space. I knew that nothing I could say (as an outsider) would convince these women that this new center was a

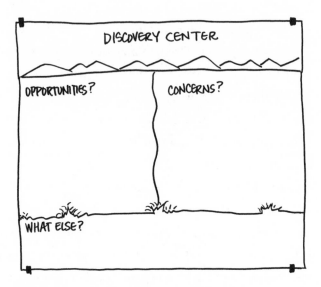

good idea. And, as I stood there and reflected on the other conversations we had had in the community, I recalled that people had been optimistic and yet still reserved. I realized then and there that getting the women of the community to buy into the concept would truly provide the green light for going forward.

As the team quietly let the women think through the idea and the concept, an older woman from the back of the room asked a very simple question: "Do you think that if we have this center, we will get fresher produce here? More choices at the store?" I replied, "I honestly don't know. What do you think?" At this point this woman shared with her neighbors her concerns about not having healthy food choices for her family available in the town. She went on to say that a center like the one we were describing would mean that the stores would have to carry fresher food and ultimately more variety in order to please visitors. She also suggested that perhaps a place like the center might bring their children home after they went to college or university because there would be the promise of a good job and something interesting to do at home.

It was as if a floodgate had been opened. The women began talking excitedly about the possibilities, their concerns, the curriculum, and the programs. The scheduled one-hour meeting went to 1½ hours, with many new ideas being shared and guidance being given on family and after-school programs that had not been previously discussed. The team had alignment in the room, and we had the group's agreement to move forward. For such an important project, there was trust, with a key stakeholder group being willing to participate beyond a focus group meeting. Having all of these conditions was like adding fuel to a fire. Janet Ross reflected, "Community buy-in is the only way this project will succeed. Whatever is the 'hook' for buy-in, that's what makes people see its potential and support its success." The community buy-in was the accelerant for this project, and it took off. Monticello's hands-on discovery center is set up to achieve its vision of new buildings, a research facility, an astronomical observatory, and much more. To learn more about this project, visit www.fourcornersschool.org/canyon-country-discovery-center.

Using the three principles and pictures together accelerates commitment and buy-in and produces real results. Many people describe this as the magic that happens when they engage in a visual strategy process. As long as the three principles have been deployed thoughtfully and with attention to including multiple stakeholders, there comes a moment when the energy in the room shifts away from the past and toward the future. *Acceleration* is the outcome of conditional convergence, and it quickly converts pictures and strategies into drivers of action, change, and success. "Why does this happen?" and "How does it happen?" are legitimate questions to ask. Exploring these two questions holds the key to what fuels a plan beyond strategy into the domain of execution.

Why does this happen? Acceleration can be defined as "a measure of how fast velocity changes." This is a physical definition from the real world—how the speed of something changes, right? And the measures that we use over time can be seen in value added or money, in actual speed (think of a race car), or in how quickly someone changes a behavior or changes his mind. We apply the meaning of acceleration in business when we talk about "just-in-time manufacturing," meaning how fast can a business get my customized product to me? We also apply it with regard to "change readiness," when we assess the ability of a culture to change and at what rate. In all these cases, we want to know the speed and rate of change within a system, a culture, a team, or even a business. We want to create the ideal conditions for people and their systems to speed up, change course, and get on a new path. But it gets even more interesting.

There is also something known as the *accelerator effect*. This is described as "the phenomenon that a variable moves toward its desired value faster and faster with respect to time." For example, in economics, the accelerator effect occurs when an economy has full employment, consumer confidence, and capital investment. These conditions contribute to the overall effect of accelerating growth in the economy. When the same variables are out of balance or not working together, the opposite occurs—deceleration.

The meaning of acceleration and the accelerator effect coincides with the way maps are an accelerator when we are picturing and executing a strategy. The images, colors, metaphors, and key words are the series of variables that work together to produce movement in a direction that yields a result. We need to have all of the following in place in a series of maps (or in one) and visually portrayed:

- A system that agrees on the direction it should take

- People who are clear about what matters most in their complex systems and how to focus on the things that matter

- Individuals and teams that are excited about the possibilities and can "see" them in moving toward them

- A system that maintains the confidence, trust, and commitment needed to sustain performance-related activity

This has an accelerator effect. To put it simply, employees move faster and faster toward something they want. They portray this through the pace of their conversations and the tone of their voices when they talk about the possibilities and opportunities. There is a slight collective euphoric feeling (think giddy) and a level of excitement that something new is happening. The feeling is contagious. This is also the result of the accelerator effect—positive conditions continue to present themselves over and over again. Everyone wants to be engaged; they are excited about what's happening, and they feel that they are a part of what is being discussed and planned. In Sean's story, remember how Charlie wanted to include his team in the second meeting? He said the team members were curious about what had happened when the senior management team went to an off-site and wanted the same thing that the senior team had had with Daniel.

"The excitement of the possibility of expressing myself and contributing is bigger than the fear I might have about being inadequate or less capable. People rise to the occasion, and they do so with joy! The work is real, it's relevant, it's a good process, and I can see the results of deliberation, disagreement, resolution, and alignment in the visual. The picture connects the joy and the work," reflected Carlos Mota as he discussed why pictures have become an important way for him to work.

Similarly, in an interview with business consultant, artist, and intuitive coach Jeraldene Lovell-Cole, she commented, "I have seen many instances in business where things are changing and new ideas for moving forward are being discussed. When the ideas, questions, and possible solutions are captured in images as they emerge in the room, a sense of ownership arises. Participants see they are really being listened to, as their suggestions are recorded on the 'map.' This encourages real alignment with possible solutions. People are truly engaged, and you don't have to push 'buy-in.' Large-scale visuals like this provide organizations with a blueprint that is 'alive' because it captures the energy in the room. This blueprint serves as a plan, a structure, a way to do the work. Their energy is also embodied in the map. These ingredients create engagement, which is critical to getting things done." The level of engagement matches people's emotional, physical, and intellectual commitment. When energy is high and the clarity and purpose are pictured, people will let go of old ways of working and get into the new "picture." When whole cultures or business systems do this, it is transformational. Acceleration provides the velocity that enables the system to move, and move it does.

As we examine how acceleration works, we know that the three principles go a long way toward creating the right conditions to transform decision making and business strategy. Using the three principles and a visual in the context of a large multinational business where these activities are not the norm may prove a bigger challenge. In the *Harvard Business Review* article "Accelerate!," John Kotter discusses the need for real business strategy in a world that is constantly changing. As described earlier, globalization, product relevance, and relationships with customers put unique demands on business leaders. Kotter maintains that as organizations get bigger and even more risk averse, they lose their abilities and the time to strategically respond to opportunity or adversity. Agility, flexibility, and responsiveness are elusive in hierarchical organizations that are focused on day-to-day business, maintaining their market share, and generating profits.

Kotter asks us to consider a business structure that allows for two systems. These two systems "operate in concert" with each other. There is an operating system (or "management-driven hierarchy") and a "strategy system" or "strategy network." The strategy network includes people from all functions and levels within the business. A guiding coalition leads the strategy network, and a set of guiding principles provides the governance needed to achieve results. He argues that the benefit of a separate system is that while the network coordinates activity with the operating system, the hierarchical rules and conventional ways of working do not apply to the network, thus allowing members of the business to respond and react differently to opportunities that might otherwise fail to be considered.

The formal creation of a strategy network that coexists alongside the operational side of the business is revolutionary. The concept provides a clever way to bridge what we have today (a hierarchical system that is slow to respond) and agility in the form of a strategy-focused social network that is in charge of going viral within the business it serves.

Kotter's strategy network formalizes the conditions required for the successful design and implementation of strategy. It puts into place the systems and structures that are needed to respond to the rapid-fire challenges and opportunities facing business every day but are lacking within large systems. With everyone in the network seen as a leader, with everyone being considered a catalyst for change, and with everyone having the authority and ability to leverage others, the conditions for success are replicated over and over again—the accelerator effect. This becomes a ripe landscape for transforming the types of decisions that business leaders and managers make and how they make them.

There is one thing missing from Kotter's proposal: pictures, images, and metaphors that connect the two systems and tie them to each other. Large-scale maps of what is being responded to and why would begin to provide a blueprint that would validate the activities of the strategy network. In the operational system, leaders and

RESULTS!

OPERATIONAL
SYSTEM

"STRATEGY
NETWORK."

employees could "see" what the strategy network is doing and how it is trickling into the day-to-day business. Remember, building and supporting one another's pictures builds shared understanding and relationships. The kind of pictures created by the two systems separately and together would help leaders see the connections between strategy and operation on multiple levels. Large-scale pictures of how the network works with and for the operating system would ease the fear coming from those people who are anxious or distrustful of such a network and a new way of working. If there are operational or strategic gaps as the two systems work together, the visuals would reveal these gaps and let leaders and members know where to focus their time and attention. Finally, leaders would be able to see the quick wins as the two systems used visual language to make meaning of their actions, their interactions, and their results for the organization.

Kotter's innovation creates a palatable solution for companies that are willing to experiment and take a chance on a new, simultaneous system that addresses a deficit in current business practice. Kotter summarizes, "The inevitable failures of single operating systems hurt us now. They are going to kill us in the future. The 21st century will force us all to evolve toward a fundamentally new form of organization. . . . Nevertheless, the companies that get there first, because they act now, will see immediate and long-term success—

for shareholders, customers, employees, and themselves. Those that lag will suffer greatly, if they survive at all."

Based on the work in strategic illustration, graphic recording, and graphic visualization, I predict that the use of images and pictures will create tighter connections between the two systems, producing faster results. I can even imagine organizations being able to move easily and seamlessly between the two systems to the point where they would not need two systems. The two systems would effectively become one. With pictures at the core of their work, an organizational structure could emerge that uniquely meets the needs of the business and supports the style of work and delivery. With a system that continues to support and provide conditions for success, acceleration becomes the norm for the large-scale multinational businesses that Kotter mentions, so that instead of living in the past, they respond to a future of possibilities. After all, the future is calling now.

CHAPTER 6

T his whole book has been leading up to this moment—the moment when you confront the voice in your head that says, "This makes pretty good sense," and the other voice that says, "What, are you crazy? You can't do that!"

I believe the world is moving into a period in which using pictures, metaphors, and words is going to be the norm when it comes to business strategy, planning, and innovation. We will see more and more organizations of all sizes embracing the idea that a good picture combined with a great strategy will travel throughout the organization and inspire, motivate, and move people to action. We have examined the business environment, and we have used stories and examples to explain when pictures work and why they make sense. Are you inspired? And, are you still a bit nervous? That's okay—this chapter is for you.

In this chapter, we focus on two "whens" and a "what": *When* should I use drawing? *When* are pictures most useful as a strategy tool? And, finally, *what* do I draw? This provides more guidance and a specific focus on how you might use drawing every day at work and in business, maybe for the rest of your life. The ultimate aim is for you to understand and feel comfortable with the idea that pictures are there to strategically support your success and the success of your business.

Let's start by discussing the two whens.

WHEN SHOULD I USE DRAWING?

You should use drawing all the time. Why? I have a long list of reasons, but here, I believe, are the main reasons why anyone who is in business should draw. And, there are others who feel this way.

Drawing helps you see things you might not otherwise see. I interviewed a CEO of a multinational company who uses pictures in his work with his company and his teams. Before every meeting with any group (customers, the board of directors, the senior leadership team), he takes a sheet of blank, unlined paper and draws an image of what he wants out of the meeting in the upper left-hand corner. He leaves the other three-quarters of the page blank and takes it into the meeting with him. "I always have my outcome in plain view. The rest of the paper is so that I can try to see what everyone else sees," he shared. "I draw what they are talking about on the rest of the paper to listen and to understand. This helps me see the whole picture and make new connections. I understand where they are coming from."

Left-brain/right-brain exercise. If for no other reason, you should draw because it slows you down, allowing you to use both sides of your brain to see nonlinear things in an organized and structured way. It also challenges you to find connections and relationships among spreadsheets, charts, people, structures, and data in creative ways.

New systems and structures arise out of drawing. When you organize your thoughts visually, you use different symbols to represent many things. Todd Barker, senior partner at Meridian Institute, shared, "I draw in my home office to help organize my thinking. I think more people should use this as an organizing tool because all the people we work with have different ways of processing information. If I hit a roadblock with a colleague and I can share something visually with him, it can help get past the differences we see and focus on the common ground."

Drawing can change how you make decisions. Drawing what they see, hear, and observe changes the way business leaders and their employees interact with one another, and how they interact with the information required to take action. Making a critical business decision with only a few pieces of information can be a disaster. Drawing all the variables involved in a decision, showing the connections among those variables, and picturing various scenarios to determine the impact on them can quickly provide business leaders and their staffs with critical connections and information that they need to make a good and calculated business decision.

When you draw, your attention is shifted toward what you are drawing. If you have a difficult topic to raise or a controversial issue to resolve, drawing can be a great way to put distance between you and the issue. When you draw, say Mikael Krogerus and Roman Tschäppeler in *The Decision Book,* "Attention is directed from your person to your subject. You are no longer standing in front of a jury, you are speaking with the jury about a separate issue." They go further and state, "Images are always remembered in connection with feelings and places. Your listeners will look at the model and remember your lecture."

Drawing supports enhanced listening. One of the challenges with the fast-paced, high-demand work environments that we have to deal with today is that our listening skills have deteriorated. People either formulate a response to someone before that person has finished her statement, or are distracted by technology and other "conversations" that are happening at the same time. When an individual sits and draws with a pencil, a few colors, and a piece of paper, it quiets the brain just enough to bring a focus on what is being said so that the individual can pay attention to it and participate in a discussion.

Practice makes perfect. Sports, music, and art have all taught us that the more we do something, the better we get at it. In my experience, we all want to draw. From people who take strategic illustration courses to those same people in meetings where pictures are being used, we *want* to do it. It goes back to our deep desire to create. So go ahead and give in to the desire. Try it and your colleagues will admire you for your courage, your team will believe you when you talk about "old dogs learning new tricks," and you will find unique ways to talk, work, and create with people in the workplace. You will have more fun, guaranteed! Which brings me to my last point.

Draw together. "Drawing together brings things down to the 'human scale'—a scale that is intimate in size and is drawn by hand. Human relationships are enhanced through the new connections these drawings make between people and what's important to them," offers Juanita Brown, cofounder of the World Café.

We have discussed the need to find new ways to connect to one another that go beyond just written or verbal. Drawing together creates a level of safety (you aren't in it alone) and pushes us to think about ideas and challenges in the context of the person or group we are drawing with. As businesses around the world fight to hold onto customers and talent, I believe we will see more teams and organizations supporting the use of pictures as a way to think about key issues and work in the future. It's one medium that we all have in common—a visual language.

WHEN ARE PICTURES MOST USEFUL AS A STRATEGY TOOL?

This is an excellent question. There are times when a picture of your strategy is not as useful as it would be at other times. Picturing your business strategy can be useful when you consider how businesses actually make things happen to deliver a product or service to a customer. I call this the *strategy-execution continuum.*

All aspects of business fall along this continuum, from marketing and sales to business strategy, finance, and budget. Whether you are a start-up with a new idea or a multinational corporation with business on each of the seven continents, business professionals at your organization use intuition and similar approaches to planning, strategy, and execution. As professionals, we get, acquire, or generate great ideas; we develop a plan to make those ideas happen (or prove that we should not make them happen); and we move forward to execute that plan, producing a new service, product, or process. This happens millions of times every day with sole proprietors, multinational businesses, and cross-functional teams. Where can pictures be most useful across this continuum and help business leaders and their teams get to execution more quickly?

Large-scale maps and pictures of a team's thinking and planning fit nicely into many parts of the strategy-execution continuum. The following suggestions are examples of formats for different stages of the continuum. The list begins with idea generation and works its way through to structuring, organizing, and executing an idea, product, or service.

Dreaming, idea sharing, or brainstorming map. The purpose of this map is to get all the ideas into one place. The more people who participate in this idea "storming," the better. Icons and color can be used to group certain items so that people can see the common elements across the ideas. Some ideas may be more operational, others may be marketing, and still others are related to customers. The colors and icons help to organize and make meaning of the "storming" activity.

Vision, outcome, or purpose map. Once possibilities have been brainstormed, this map helps to define the team's direction or purpose. A question that a team may use to guide its conversation is, "What do we hope to gain through this effort?" This question focuses on defining the outcome or purpose. Another question would be, "What are we driving at?" The answer to this question clarifies the genesis of the original idea and begins

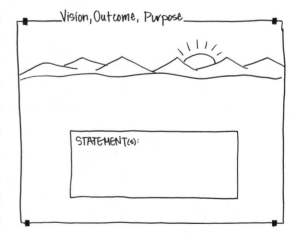

to focus on the outcome, vision, goal, or purpose that the team hopes to accomplish.

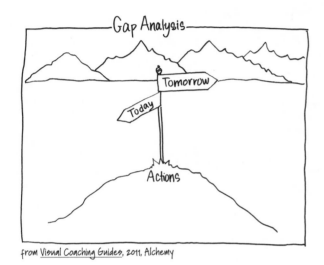

from <u>Visual Coaching Guides</u>, 2011, Alchemy

Gap analysis map. This template helps portray where a new idea, solution, or change fits within the existing structure. The team uses this tried-and-true business model to define what is happening today and where the business could be tomorrow. The visual template at the center is the "crossroads" between today and tomorrow. Team members should ask themselves, "What specific actions can we take today to get closer to where we want to be?" Then fill that in here.

Focus group or customer/stakeholder feedback map. Using a picture to capture customer or stakeholder ideas dealing with opportunities or concerns that they see in a new product, service, or business idea is invaluable. Doing this visually, using the same template over and over again with different groups of people (different ages, demographics, geographic representation, and so on), can provide rich intelligence that reveals many levels of information. The facilitation that accompanies this template is dynamic and can be as open-ended or as focused as needed. It elicits everything from an emotional reaction to a product or service to the legal, operational, and financial consequences of moving forward with a product or service.

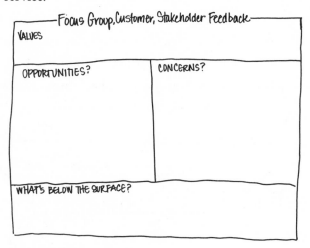

Road map with benchmarks. As a business idea matures, a road map can provide a distillation of the direction in which you are moving and the necessary milestones or benchmarks needed to achieve the final goal as you and your team see it. This map can also be modified to show how different "roads" can be used to achieve the same outcome; this can be a great tool for contingency planning.

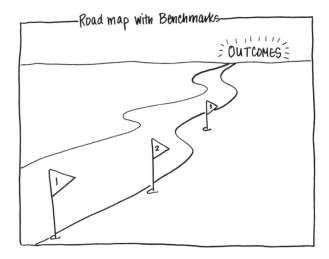

Project activity map. This map simply captures the main business categories (like sales, marketing, operations, and personnel) that need to be involved and the associated activities that need to be carried out to get a product or service to market. Activities are organized by using similar icons and the same color in each main category. While this type of map is fairly straightforward, its basics can be highly customized and changed to accommodate the specific scenarios and systems needed to launch the product.

Strategic action planning. This is a full-blown action planning map that includes strategic priorities on the left-hand side of the map; key actions and activities organized by the quarter in which they will get done; and goals and measures on the far right-hand side to drive activities toward the final goal, which includes measurement and results. Inspired by *The Balanced Scorecard* by Robert

S. Kaplan and David P. Norton (1996), this business model delivers specific actions that can be measured and, based on your organizational culture, can be further cascaded into the specific priority areas as well.

Strategic Action Planning

PRIORITIES	ACTIVITIES BY QUARTER	GOALS + MEASURES
1		★ ★
2		★ ★
3		★ ★
4		★ ★
5		★ ★

As you move through the stages of dreaming and brainstorming, vision or purpose, and activity planning, pictures of your strategy are extremely useful. Since the ideas have not been solidly formed (at least in the early stages), there are multiple opportunities to discuss the ideas with various people inside and outside the business. The pictures become a way to talk about a new product or service without going into so much detail that you overwhelm those with whom you are consulting. The examples provided here are intentionally simple. They allow multiple perspectives and categories to be added, changed, or modified based on what works best for a particular business situation across the strategy-execution continuum. Think of these templates as guides to jump-start a "creating" process. The rules are fairly straightforward: (1) Make sure that whatever you choose to do will really work for the team, business or company, and setting. (2) Experiment—the first template you use may not be the "right" one, so try something different. (3) Do not do this work in a vacuum. If you do, the results will be, well, in a vacuum.

As a business moves down the strategy-execution continuum into the activity and planning phases, picturing a business strategy is also effective. The suggested templates serve two primary purposes. First, they contain and represent all the collective thinking, reflection, and conversations that were part of the effort that led up to the planning map you settled on. Effective planning and activity maps contain and project how the group or team will get from one place to another place in the future. In an interview with author, artist, and business consultant Ulric Rudebeck about his work with pictures, strategy, and business, he offered, "These [activity] maps combine time, content, and the physical condition or space for the team. They tell us what is going to happen (content) over what period of time and toward what end or what opportunity (space). These planning maps are a synthesis and a realization of what the team set out to accomplish in its earlier planning stages."

The map templates and processes that are closer to the execution end of the continuum become more like production "blueprints" of activity and accountability. Changes and modifications can be made to them (and frequently are) based on variables that the team has no control over, such as changes in markets, weather, technology disruption, or late delivery. Accountability to the team and the business is thrust forward on these "blueprints" by the level of specificity, the identification of who will do the work, and the demonstration of commitment. These are more often referred to as action planning maps. Team members frequently sign their names to the map as an outward and official display of commitment and acknowledgment that this is the agreed-upon path forward.

As the team or the business focuses on executing its plans, large-scale visuals like those discussed become less useful. The focus at this stage of the continuum is on *doing* the work you have been planning for and delivering value to the firm. There are examples of manufacturing teams using large-scale visuals to interpret or synthesize Six Sigma data; while useful, these maps are largely disposable because the point of them is to identify something that is not working, create a solution to course-correct, make that correction, and move on. Any maps that are done this close to or in relation to execution are also disposable. They often help teams understand what is holding them back or what they need to do to make a breakthrough, or reveal a pattern that needs to change as they get closer to attaining their goal.

Some companies laminate or frame their strategy maps as a way to keep the business focus in that direction. The pictures of a business strategy remain useful as a reminder of what people are focusing on and why. Other organizations use the pictures as a talking point for orienting new employees or sharing their organizational strategy with customers. They retain the energy, focus, and enthusiasm that went into creating them. I recall visiting a manufacturing plant site of one of my clients almost two years after an intense set of strategy sessions with that client. The first map was still up on the wall above the doors that led into the production area. People I met for the first time pointed to the map and shared with me how they had learned about the story captured there. The general manager commented on how important that map had been to the repositioning of the business. Anyone who knew the history of the business was deeply attached to the images that the map portrayed. New employees came into a culture that embraced the vision, principles, and guidance that had been created by their peers.

It would be great if all production and delivery were really this simple: create a strategy and go through the various phases to get to execution, delivery, and value creation. However, the context in which we deliver value in business casts a new light on our business and our work. We execute on products, goods, or services in the context of human relationships, power, politics, price, economic conditions, regulation, hierarchy, competition, and other threats to our business.

When I think of these conditions and how they influence work, there is another continuum that exerts influence on business systems.

I call this the *clarity-complexity continuum*. One end of our business activity is clear (clarity). We know what we need to do, our goal is in sight, and we go after it. At the other end of the continuum is complexity. This involves factors that influence and intensify our workplace. These elements create confusion, frustration, and miscommunication and contribute to low trust and lack of alignment. Illuminating complexity at the right level within organizations is important to enabling the team or the business to execute and deliver value.

What type of pictures can be used across this continuum? While clarity may not need a specific picture per se to support your strategy, something that is simple, bold, and colorful can help everyone in the business remember the clear purpose, focus, deliverable, or outcome.

As we move across this continuum *from* clarity *toward* complexity, some ideas for pictures may include the following:

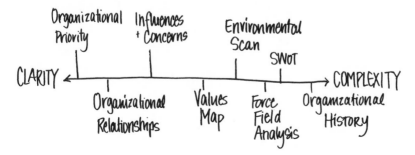

Organizational priority map. This is truly the view from "above" and a perfect template for senior teams who are responsible for multiple programs and projects. These teams have a deep need to see everything in one space. It is immensely gratifying to see all the dynamics and projects in one place where you can read them (rather than in a 10-point font!). Abandon the desire to have too much detail in this map, as the goal is to see the interrelationships among programs and projects, identify what the priorities are based on a set of opportunities and challenges, and use this visual to identify what gets done first, second, and so on.

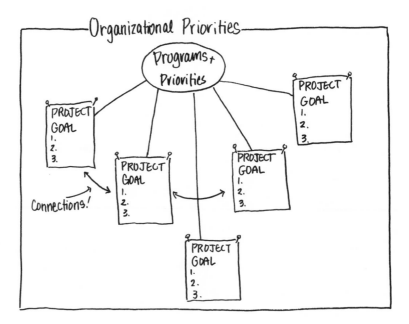

Organizational relationship map. Similar to an organizational chart, this map identifies who has influence, responsibility, and accountability for a product, challenge, or division in your organization. This template is useful when a team needs to identify individuals in the business who could make a difference or who have influence that could assist with the product or an envisioned system change. In this map, the team members identify the relationships they have; the relationships they want, explaining why; and the relationships they need in order to support the plan or idea going forward. The map can also include how the team plans to get the necessary people on board and by what time.

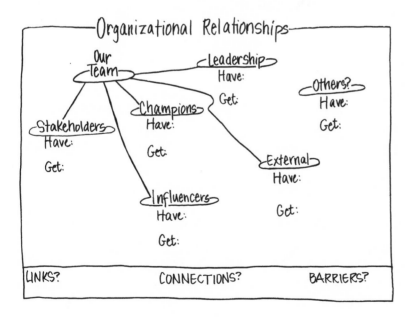

Influence and concern map. Borrowing from Stephen Covey's work (*7 Habits of Highly Effective People*, 1989), this map helps illuminate what a team or a group of people is *concerned* about in the business and distinguish that from what the people involved actually have *influence* over. This type of map can clarify what the people involved can do with the influence they have, and what things they are concerned about they might need to let go of. Letting go of things that the team is concerned about, but that it lacks the influence and authority to bring about, helps create focus on what actions are needed to get a job done.

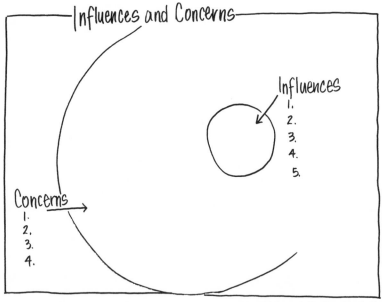

from 7 Habits of Highly Effective People

Values map. Mapping the organizational values (stated or real) along with the values of the individuals on the team can help delineate what's important to whom and why. It also shows how the organizational values fit with the values of the individuals and the team. This map can also catalyze conversations about how the behaviors that are grounded in these values are helping or hurting productivity and the business now. As part of this map, people frequently ask their team, "What needs to change in order for us to deliver the kind of performance we dream about?"

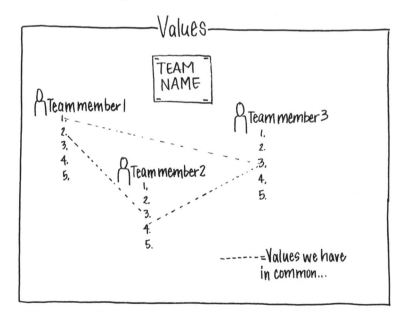

Environmental scan. I advocate using the traditional business model with pictures to really see what impact external influences

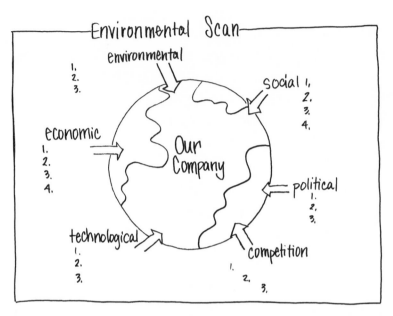

(social, political, environmental, economic, technological, and competition) are having on you, your team, and your business. Done visually, this exercise can provide new insights, connections among the external forces, and information about the competition that was not previously seen. As discussed earlier, be courageous about the questions you ask during this process because they will yield additional information about the business and the competition that goes beyond the superficial.

Force field analysis. This simple concept is a powerful way to illuminate what changes in behavior and actions are needed to drive toward success. Three simple questions are asked: "What are the

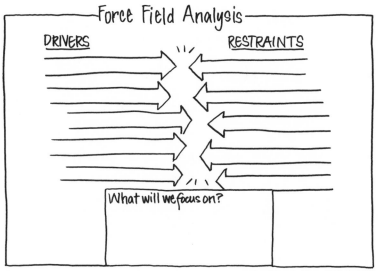

from Kurt Lewin's Force Field Analysis

things already in place that are helping us drive toward our goal(s) and success?" "What are things that we believe are holding us back, restraining us from attaining out goal(s)?" And finally, "What will we do to place more focus on the things that are driving our success and less focus on the things that are holding us back?"

SWOT (strengths, weaknesses, opportunities, and threats) analysis. This is another relevant and standard business strategy approach. When this analysis is done in pictures, amazing metaphors emerge that help team members see the same thing (especially their strengths and the opportunities in the business). Pictures also allow everyone to see what pressures from the external environment (threats and opportunities) might influence performance today and envision the kind of performance that is needed in the future.

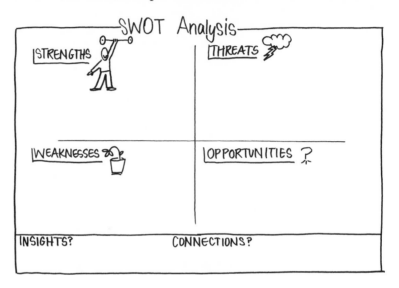

Organizational history map. "History is like a container. . . . It is a well to draw from in order to understand. It gives perspectives on what has happened and it shows the principles and patterns for how things can evolve. . . . This phase is an archeological search," offers Ulric Rudebeck in *Strategic Vision Work*. The history of a business is diverse, full of myth, controversy, truths, stories, and invaluable information about complexity and patterns. Using a full-blown history map can reveal different patterns, beliefs, and values involving an organization. History maps typically reflect the intellectual, political, social, and market dynamics within the company and can explain how it came to be where it is at that moment. Often, this high-impact visual alone can bring a level of clarity about what an organization needs to do in order to move in a different direction and begin to build new patterns.

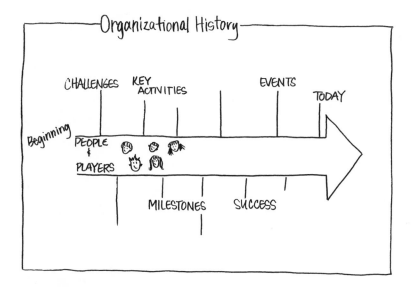

As organizations, leaders, and their people move along the clarity-complexity continuum, pictures make this process more productive and more relevant to the business. Too often, this continuum gets confused with the "soft stuff" in business. Yes, it is soft because it is about people and how they work. And these are the very behaviors and attitudes that can sabotage a new product or prevent action from happening. When pictures are used to help illuminate some of the confusion that exists, the team members can engage and can begin to feel the movement toward clarity. They begin to see the possibilities that come with clarity and focus.

The point of a picture, which works anywhere along this continuum, is to give meaning and language to the things that get in the way of outstanding performance. Pictures in a strategy context give people a choice about what to keep and what to leave behind as they embrace a new story, new patterns, and new business. Pictures allow everyone to talk about the choices, the direction, and their role in the future. When planning for strategy work using visuals, Ulric Rudebeck shares, "All the pictures capture, keep together, and transfer the ideas, experiences, feelings and thoughts between people. It is also the form in which you save complex ideas and relationships so you can tell them again. . . . It is through the pictures . . . that people's minds open to a new way of thinking. They dare to think the unthinkable and they invent a new alternative future."

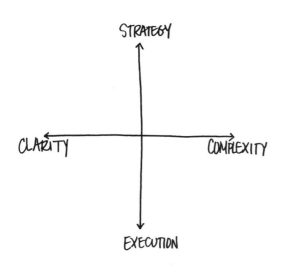

As we bring these two continua together, where do we see businesses spending most of their time? I believe we think we spend the majority of our time in the box between clarity and execution. In reality, most companies, large and small, in any industry, spend a good percentage of their time in the space between complexity and strategy. We need to know where we should go and why we are going there. We will go in that direction when there is a level of clarity of purpose and direction. As we gain clarity and move toward execution, trust improves, alignment occurs, and business quickly moves into executing strategy.

What happens when the two continua intersect, and where do they intersect? Visually speaking, you hit the strategy jackpot—the bull's-eye! Visuals that guide, support, and contain the strategy and planning while capturing the complexity create *conditional convergence*—a tipping point that propels a shift. This is when a team that is working through a deep planning process moves in a different direction. The intersection of these two continua is where and when that shift occurs. How do we know that there has been a shift?

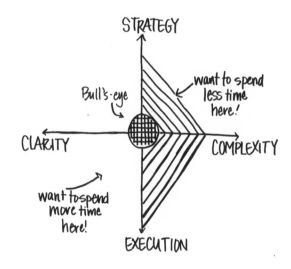

Lois Todd, senior partner at Alchemy and a neuro-linguistic programming (NLP) master practitioner, identified the shift when the language in the room changes from "I" or "mine" to "we" or "ours." According to Lois, "This happens when the people in the room find the right metaphor that describes the new ways they want to work together and the new direction they are working toward. When this happens, what people say is different from what they were saying before. Someone on the team suggests a metaphor that resonates with the whole group, and the room explodes. People talk excitedly about what they see and how it will work in the organization—not for the individual. People speak easily about what 'we' are going to do and why. There is an ease and joy that carries ideas, commitment, and action forward. It is like magic."

The whole point of picturing a business strategy is to get closer to seamless execution with clarity, focus, direction, and success. Tools or practices that bring a level of clarity and focus are usually embraced by the leadership (even skeptics). Processes and tools that strengthen systems and structures to sustain execution and delivery are coveted by even the most conservative companies. Who doesn't like double-digit growth year after year? The shift described here can be painful, complicated, and hard. It breaks the organization's old patterns. However, it does get easier as people practice new ways of working with strategy and execution. An authentic tipping point, one that makes a lasting change, is a result of hard work, commitment from the leadership, listening carefully to multiple and diverse stakeholders, and the courage to make a change. The pictures provide a container for all of this, both good and bad. They help members of the team who are stuck, and they help others figure out how the future looks different. Images and metaphors also identify what needs to change and develop a new language where work and change come together.

WHAT DO I DRAW?

The templates described earlier are just the beginning of picturing *your* business strategy. They provide an organized way to think about how to use pictures that makes sense for your business. While there is no "right" or "wrong" template, you can relax and know that many professionals across the globe have used all of these with their clients. The key to finding the right template is to experiment. Try modifying and changing the things in these or other templates to make them work. Don't be afraid to let go of a visual idea or image that you love, because it may not really work with your team or your business. You will get better at understanding what you draw as you practice and take chances with different icons and different templates. Experimentation and "trying" will help you land on what works best for you.

In strategic illustration classes, I encourage people to explore using other things that are out there that help them get familiar and comfortable with using visual language at work. Copying works best. Comic books, visual novels, and cartoons are a good place to start. There are also companies that specialize in supporting people who want to use pictures to create their business strategy. Grove Consultants International (www.grove.com), based in San Francisco, has a plethora of templates that you can purchase online or that can be mailed directly to you in multiple formats (large-scale, flipchart, or smaller sizes). Grove has partners throughout Europe that also work with it, so if that feels like a safer place to start, visit its website. Another place to find great ideas for things that might work with your team is Neuland (www.neuland.com), which has distribution throughout Europe, Canada, and the United States. Its visual icon books, posters, and moderation resources can support almost any process you want to design and execute. Your imagination is your only limitation. Other references, resources, and guides are listed in Appendix A.

In addition to the templates described here to picture your strategy, there are other simple things you can draw.

Icons. These are small symbols that give a visual anchor to key concepts that you use in your business again and again. Settle on your "top 10 icons" and always have them in your "back pocket" ready to use and draw. One of the "alchemists" who took my class photographed her top 10 icons and has them on her smartphone, ready to use. Make sure you include them in a sketchbook for note taking and use them on a flipchart, a whiteboard, or a large piece of paper. Once your team or your employees have seen those icons more than three times, they will begin to visually organize their agendas, discussions, and action items relative to those icons. Another professional who took my class shared this: "Lightbulbs now mean ideas, arrows mean actions, and conversation bubbles mean

A NOTE ABOUT HANDWRITING

People say all the time, "I have such messy handwriting." First of all, slow down. Your printing will improve when you take your time. Second, don't try to write and look at the audience at the same time. People can't do a good job of printing the letters while they are looking at the audience—the letters slant either upward or downward and look messy. This is not the picture that you want people to leave with. People are patient, and they will look at your back for just a moment so that you can make your writing neat and legible. They may be anxious about what you are writing, but like a surprise, you can make it look beautiful.

discussion. These images appear on our agenda every week instead of numbers or letters. Everyone knows what they stand for."

Words. Words can be like pictures; you can draw the word "apple" the way it actually looks, or you can print the word in a style that conveys emotion or emphasis. You can combine words with icons, and this will focus the meaning of the word and the image in that direction. As adults, we first process words, then tap into our visual repertoire. Words are the way to anchor key concepts in our pictures,

and they bring greater meaning to the overall picture. You don't have to write out full sentences. Just focus on one to three words that summarize what's being said. This summary combined with the image will help people remember what is being said, why it was said, and even how it was said.

People. Are you freaking out?! Relax. People are hard to draw, but thankfully, we do not need to draw them in vivid detail. Stick figures and bubble heads are just fine. "You can only draw stick-men? Not to worry. The more sophisticated and perfect a drawing is, the more alienating it is. With simple, clear drawings the audience gets the feeling that they could do this too," comment Krogerus and Tschäppeler in *The Decision Book*. You have to draw people. No negotiation. The reason? Because we work with people, not icons. It's people in businesses and organizations that we are trying to communicate with, engage, and inspire. People have to see themselves as part of the picture, and trust me, they will get it. You just did when you saw the images given here, right?

Frames. Putting a frame around something contains it. When you look at something framed, your brain focuses on what is framed compared with the things around it. We calm down and reflect. What's inside the frame looks organized. Think of any picture in your home and how it looked before it was framed. How does it look now? When it's framed, it is finished and presentable.

Framing something also creates a physical separation between me and whatever is in that frame. I can point to it, refer to it, and invite others to work in that frame, but I am separate from whatever is in there. This can be helpful when teams disagree about direction, focus, and details and you are helping to facilitate a conversation that needs to move from disagreement to consensus and, ultimately, action.

Color. This is one of the easiest and best ways to organize information and show off your new drawing skills. Alternating colors on a flipchart is a great place to start. Again, this brings some structure to the way things are listed on the chart. The color breaks things up for the viewer; it helps people remember. Put a frame around it, and voilà! You have a picture that sets a tone for what will happen during your meeting. You are on your way to picturing your strategy.

These lines...

Darker colors are easier to read, so use these for words. Lighter colors are great highlights and can be used to capture emotional emphasis. If people are really excited about something, you can underline it in red. If they have a set of ideas they want to try, you can give them emphasis by using lines of expression—outlined in yellow.

If you combine these five things (icons, words, people, frames, and color) with any template or idea you have for a visual structure, you will be picturing your business strategy in no time.

Can I Draw the "Wrong" Picture?

Not if you are listening really well and are fully engaged with the people you are in conversation with. As mentioned earlier, listening is a twenty-first-century skill that we all need to be better at. Good listening will guide your hand in what you draw. If you have your own image in your head well before the conversation begins, and you are determined to draw that picture exactly the way you see it, chances are you are not listening. You run the risk of creating a picture that is *your* picture, but is not one that will allow you to fully realize the benefit of pictures in a collective business context.

Can you use your image as a conversation starter? You bet! It's a display of courage. You just need to know that in a group setting, your picture is likely to change, and it should! That's how terrific and sustainable strategies get created.

What if I Want Someone Else to Draw?

In Sean's story, Daniel played a vital role in supporting John and his senior team. He helped them create the right processes and the right pictures that resonated for the teams and were what the division needed. If you are a stakeholder, or if you want or need to be in the conversation as a participant, then I encourage you to find someone who is not a stakeholder, who is outside your team or even your business, and who can listen well and remain neutral to draw for or with you. This can be a strategic illustrator, a graphic recorder, or an artist in your area. Appendix A lists some places where you can find these professionals.

You can also engage someone who is internal to your business, but who works in another part of the firm. I know a large Middle Eastern company that has an employee who is an amazing artist, strategic illustrator, and graphic designer for the company. It uses his talents regularly to create the right templates and pictures to portray the strategy (in Arabic) for the business. People who have a command of visual language are like tour guides in a foreign country. They are a great and reliable resource, trusted listeners, and allies in your effort. They make the "strategic adventure" exciting, fun, energizing, and beautiful. You have confidence that the process will work because they know what they are doing. This is a much better feeling than the feeling you have when you end up in the wrong neighborhood in a city you have never been to.

THE EVOCATIVE OBJECT

Reflecting on when you should draw and what you should draw also means thinking strategically about how pictures can be used and why to use them. I have one more thought to offer. The pictures you create together with others tell a great deal about the business, its performance, its people and talent, its leadership, and its direction.

Without getting too "soft," these pictures contain the heart, soul, dreams, struggles, and aspirations of a group of people who are responsible for doing something with and for a company. Sean and his team went through the pain of pulling apart the pieces of his division, portraying them visually, and using them to understand how to get out of the situation the division was in. This is business, and we invest a lot in the work we do every day. Picturing your strategy, when it is done with integrity and authenticity, can be an emotional process. When you stick with the process and trust your intuition, supported by your imagination, the pictures will strengthen relationships and build new forms of trust that are invaluable building blocks for performance. Your pictures provide a light on the future and show the direction in which the company is headed. People literally become part of the map, the images, and the direction that is portrayed there.

"When you are moving toward the change and transformation your ideas are leading you into, the maps get populated with the people, the ideas, and the energy of those who create as well as those who come into the story after the fact. It becomes a living document and lives on. People see what they have created—the picture validates that for us, and somehow it makes the change easier to move into," shared Elizabeth Groginsky on the pictures she has used to create coalitions, define new businesses, and mobilize people to work together.

If pictures in business create a certain level of ease when moving from one direction to another, then it is not unreasonable to assume that these maps will take on a life of their own. They are infused with emotion, pride, and connection. It is not uncommon for people to get attached to an object that represents an accomplishment, an achievement, or a moment in their life. Large-scale maps are no exception, and the people who get attached to them are not just individuals—they are teams, divisions, and even whole businesses.

Sherry Turkle, a scholar from MIT and director of the MIT Initiative on Technology and Self in the Program in Science, Technology, and Society, speaks directly to the power of objects in her collection of essays *Evocative Objects*: "We think with the objects we love; we love the objects we think with." Turkle goes on to share, "With different metaphors, each describes a dynamic relationship between things and thinking. We tie a knot and find ourselves in partnership with string in our exploration of space. *Objects are able to catalyze self-creation*." Through her research and studies, Turkle finds that it is impossible to separate thought and feeling in our relationships to things—physical objects take on a meaning for us that goes beyond their physical presence. We upload thoughts, feelings, emotions,

STRATEGY

CLARITY ← → COMPLEXITY

EXECUTION

EVOCATIVE OBJECT

and ideas into metaphors and objects like the pictures we create together for our business.

Assuming that objects, like our pictures, evoke things that we hold dear, then the vulnerabilities, strengths, aspirations, and fears of employees and businesses are represented by the maps they create. The images, words, and output are intimate and important to both the individual and the business. The pictures also bind people to one another in their work—their strategy and their execution. It is no wonder that in a business context, the pictures of strategy become evidence of success; they are tangible objects to be proud of and things to willingly share with others because they are objects that represent the individual and collective story.

Like most objects that are treasured personally, these pictures move when people move—they travel. Picturing a business strategy is a way to take that strategy and the experience of creating it, the picture, with you wherever you go. I love images and business strategies that travel. What do I mean by travel? Think about iconic buildings or symbols that have transcended their actual meaning and represent other things. For example, imagine the Eiffel Tower in Paris. It does not matter if you have never been to Paris. It can be described, or there are pictures of it. It's pretty easy to draw (think a triangle with a little circle on top). When I show individuals a picture of the Eiffel Tower, it conjures up many things—travel, an engineering feat, romance, a foreign country, a place in France, an experience. Another example? Consider a stoplight. Regardless of where

you are in the world, red means stop and green means go. Meta-
phorically, we can use the stoplight in business for many things: a
project got the "green light"; if there is risk on the horizon, proceed
with caution—yellow.

The creation of a business strategy in pictures is an *experience*
that is not easily forgotten. When I tell people what I do in my work,
and they have experienced a planning process that included pictures,
they immediately say, "Yeah, I did that. That's cool. I still remember
some of the pictures." They then go on to share with me the context,
some of the content, and what they recall. The detail of their recol-
lection often amazes me. The experience is still alive within them.

The point is that the content, images, and metaphors are relevant, engaging, and infused with thoughtful business strategy and
people's commitment. The pictures and images are like memorable stories that we want to tell again and again—they are contagious. Like photos or videos on the Internet, the pictures go viral.
These business pictures transcend the here and now and engage audiences within that business in conversations and discussions that
go beyond the original intent or purpose of the picture. When I am
working in large multinational businesses, it is the finest compli-
ment to me and the team I am working with when someone from a
different part of the business comments, "Yeah, I saw what you created. That makes a lot of sense."

Our businesses are populated with evocative objects. Some of
them are still relevant; others are holding the space for a story, a

memory of something that happened that was important to the business. As we use more pictures in our business to build, form, and communicate our strategies, we have the ability and the tools to engage, inspire, and connect more people than any videoconference or intranet can. It really is true—if we can see it, we believe it. If we believe it, then the future that we create is already who we are. As an individual, a team, and a business, the pictures we create become a way of working and living. The maps we design become the "here" and the "now." Armed with the whole picture, we are able to respond, react, create, and thrive!

CHAPTER 7

The fall sun was shining, and it was warm on my back. The soft sound of a gurgling fountain and children playing after school could be heard in the distance. My eyes were closed; I was enjoying the peace, the quiet, and the satisfaction of a hard day's work. I had just finished one of the most rewarding and interesting meetings with 200 business leaders across France—a highlight in my professional career. My English- and French-speaking colleagues had convened a wonderful conference on innovation. They had invited thought leaders from across Europe to share interesting theories and success stories about innovation. Interspersed with the presentations were World Café conversations to help attendees plan for their own innovation back in the workplace. I assisted with the design of the conference and strategically illustrated the presentations and conversations with the help of a French colleague.

While the content of the conference was unique, the actual format and location were not what made it memorable for me. The professional highlight was the fulfillment of a lifelong dream: to work in Paris, speaking French (barely) with business professionals, and survive! Not only did I survive, but I thrived. It was one of those personal moments where everything moved with ease and grace in the direction it was supposed to. I was 100 percent present, and there was a joy to the work that was exhilarating. It was October 2008.

My mobile phone rang, and when I answered, a close friend and professional colleague was calling to find out how the conference had gone. As we chatted and I shared my satisfaction and feelings of accomplishment, he was congratulatory. He then asked if I had "heard the news." Nudged out of my revelry and remembering 9/11, I cautiously said, "What news?"

"Right, " he replied. "You've been inside all day. Don't get too satisfied with your recent success. Banks are crashing, and the global economy is headed into a recession the likes of which the world has not seen since the Great Depression." He went on to share details about banks in England, the United States, and Ireland that were close to collapse and how the world was reeling. I was distracted by my good feelings, and I honestly do not remember the rest of the conversation.

After we concluded our call, I continued to sit in the park and watch the people walk, play, talk, and enjoy the fall day. While the world was headed into a global financial crisis, these people were going about, doing what they did most days. As I reflected on my initial reaction to the "news," I remember feeling a little freaked out and scared, but the feeling did not last. Instead, what I felt was tremendous relief—relief that I had been able to fulfill a dream. I had been able to achieve something that I had always wanted to do and had never thought possible. I remember writing in a notebook that I had with me in my bag, "It does not get any better than this!" That piece of paper is now tattered and worn, but it goes everywhere with me. It reminds me of what I am passionate about and how lucky I am.

Linking my love of business strategy with pictures, images, and metaphor has made a profound difference in my life. It has affected the work I do, whom I work with, how I work, and what I create with my clients, colleagues, and friends. I cannot imagine going back to a life devoid of pictures and large-scale maps, where the rules of the game include large decks of slide presentations and enormous three-ring binders. With those days behind me, pen and paper in hand, I am more excited and challenged now that I have tools and methods that are visibly making a difference with the people and in the businesses where I work.

Over the last several years, I have observed what happens to people when they start using visuals with their business, teams, or clients. I have seen the reactions when some of the world's smartest, most talented, and most proficient business skeptics pick up a marker and stand in front of a blank piece of paper in one of the strategic illustration classes. There is an initial feeling of happiness: "This is like being a kid." Then they have trouble drawing something, and they get frustrated. As the pieces of visual language pile on top of each other, these same people become incredulous—"How can you expect anyone to do this at work? Where is the proof that this works? Where is the research?" they ask. By the second day, however, they have calmed down—they are still skeptical, but their initial anxiety has dissipated.

More believers than skeptics, they leave with their top 10 icons, a sketch pad, a permanent black marker, and a head full of ideas and colors.

With courage, anxiety, commitment, and grace, they do their first drawing with a team or a client, and the possibilities begin to unfold. "They liked it! They actually liked it! It made sense, and people were nodding, yeah—they got it!" Just as in the journey described in this book, people picture an outcome ("I can draw"), they capture complexity ("I can't draw; what was I thinking? How can I do this?"), and they create possibilities ("Look! I can do this. I will practice, and it will get easier. I will get better").

What are you waiting for? You too can live a dream—a dream that you create with a pen and paper, pictures, and images. Try it. I remain true to my word.

APPENDIX A

There are many interesting, relevant, and wonderful resources to use, to copy, and to be inspired by. This is a short list of books that we provide to people who participate in the strategic illustration courses that we teach across the United States and in Europe. Browse through them to see the many styles, ideas, and ways you can picture a business strategy.

Additional Resources and Background Information to Inspire

Lee LeFever, *The Art of Explanation: Making Your Ideas, Products, and Services Easier to Understand*

Alexander Osterwalder and Yves Pigneur, *Business Model Generation*

Tim Clark with Alexander Osterwalder and Yves Pigneur, *Business Model You*

Larry Gonick, *The Cartoon Guide to (Non) Communication: The Use and Misuse of Information in the Modern World*

Mischa Richter and Harald Bakken, *The Cartoonist's Muse: A Guide to Generating and Developing Creative Ideas*

Robin Hall, *The Cartoonist's Workbook*

Susanne F. Fincher, *Creating Mandalas*

J. E. Cirlot, *A Dictionary of Symbols*

Anna Milbourne, *Drawing Cartoons* (Internet linked)

Quentin Blake and John Cassidy, *Drawing for the Artistically Undiscovered*

Patti Dobrowolski, *Drawing Solutions: How Visual Goal Setting Will Change Your Life*

Joan Brown and Mary F. Claggett, *Drawing Your Own Conclusions: Graphic Strategies for Reading, Writing and Thinking*

Christopher Hart, *Everything You Ever Wanted to Know About Cartooning, but Were Afraid to Draw*

Richard C. Brandt, *Flip Charts: How to Draw Them and How to Use Them*

Brandy Agerbeck, *The Graphic Facilitator's Guide*

Jan V. White, *Graphic Idea Notebook*

Will Eisner, *Graphic Storytelling and Visual Narrative*

Fredrik Härén, *The Idea Book*

Charles Hampden-Turner, *Maps of the Mind: Charts and Concepts of the Mind and Its Labyrinths*

Garr Reynolds, *Presentation Zen*

Kurt Hanks and Larry Belliston, *Rapid Viz: A New Method for the Rapid Visualization of Ideas*

Larry Raymond, *Reinventing Communication: A Guide to Using Visual Language for Planning, Problem Solving, and Reengineering*

Mike Rhode, *The Sketchnote Handbook: The Illustrated Guide to Visual Notetaking*

Nancy Duarte, *Slide:ology: The Art and Science of Creating Great Presentations* (Also see www.bnet.com and enter *Duarte.*)

Robert H. McKim, *Thinking Visually: A Strategy Manual for Problem Solving*

Scott McCloud, *Understanding Comics: The Invisible Art*

David Sibbet, *Visual Meetings: How Graphics, Sticky Notes & Idea Mapping Can Transform Group Productivity* and *Visual Leaders: New Tools for Visioning Management and Organizational Change*

David McCandless, *The Visual Miscellaneum*

Edward de Bono, *Wordpower: An Illustrated Dictionary of Vital Words*

Jean Westcott and Jennifer Hammond Landau, *A Workbook for Visual Communication—A Picture's Worth a Thousand Words*

Live Animation, RSA Videos, and Strategic Animation

The whole visual world has exploded with the use of video to "livescribe" or animate hand-drawn lectures and information sessions. Thanks to Cognitive Media (www.cognitivemedia.co.uk) in the United Kingdom and its partnership with the Royal Society of the Arts (RSA Animates, www.thersa.org/events/rsaanimate), we can sit for hours and watch people draw talks and lectures. I encourage you to listen to one of these talks and draw it for practice, and then see how the illustrators at Cognitive Media did it. I bet your drawings are not so different from the ones you find online.

There are a host of drawn animation videos on YouTube that are being used by companies and organizations. Linking to some of these organizations will provide hours of fun viewing and learning how to do this yourself, with an iPad and with friends. The technology is changing so rapidly that these types of videos will soon be very affordable and the norm for most businesses—see, visuals *are* everywhere!

Other Resources About the Brain

This is another area that has exploded with information, articles, and resources to help us understand what happens between our two ears. These are favorites that were not captured in the Bibliography.

Joe Dispenza, "Evolve Your Brain: The Science of Changing Your Mind" (http://www.drjoedispenza.com/)

Joe Dispenza, *Breaking the Habit of Being Yourself*

John Medina, *Brain Rules: 12 Principles for Surviving and Thriving at Work, Home and School*

David Rock, *Your Brain at Work*

Todd Siler, *Think Like a Genius*

Where Can I Find People Who Do This? Teach It? Love It, Too?

Here are links to some organizations that help people like us connect and share insights, tips, and tricks. The organizations also maintain a list of people like me, who do this work in and with businesses around the world. There are links to conferences, blogs, animation, and videos, all of which help us deepen our practice and skill.

The Center for Graphic Facilitation
>   http://graphicfacilitation.blogs.com/pages/
International Forum for Visual Practitioners
>   http://www.ifvp.org/
>   http://survivalacademy.ning.com/
World Café
>   www.theworldcafe.com
Alchemy: The Art of Transforming Business
>   www.link2alchemy.com

Alchemy is a strategy consulting company that is passionate about creating new ways of thinking to drive business results. We take the best of business strategy and use pictures, visual images, and metaphors to engage leaders and their systems in sustainable change. These processes incorporate the latest in cognitive and brain-based science to evoke the power and potential of any company's human capital. We do this by cocreating innovative professional leadership, and cultural and business-driven experiences with and for our clients that include hosting strategic illustration and graphic facilitation courses in the United States and Europe. Bring out the alchemist in you—visualize, simplify, and prioritize. To learn more, visit our website (wwwlink2alchemy.com), stop by our headquarters in sunny Denver, Colorado, or call us at 720-932-8720.

Supplies for Your Craft

Art supplies are easy to come by. You can find most water-based and permanent pens and markers, pencils, erasers, chalk pastels, and "painter's" tape at drugstores, craft stores, art supply stores, and online. Online art supply stores in the United States (like Dick blick.com and Utrechtart.com) have vast inventories to choose from. The Grove Consultants and Neuland sell materials online throughout the United States, Canada, and Europe.

One suggestion for beginners: while it may be tempting to spend a lot of money on supplies, I encourage you to try your hand at picturing your strategy with the simplest of markers and colors. See if you like it, and then buy your markers one at a time so you can try different products. Some markers have chiseled nibs, others are pointed, and some allow you to draw with either end of the pen—one end is wide and one is small.

NOTES

Opening Quotes

page v "The smartest ideas come from those . . ." John Hunt, *The Art of the Idea* (Brooklyn, NY: Powerhouse Books, 2009), p. 129.

page v "'The only tool we have is to ride . . .'" Ulric Rudebeck, author's interview on November 12, 2012.

Introduction

page xv "Throughout 2012, *Fast Company* magazine . . ." R. Safian, "This Is Generation Flux: Meet the Pioneers of the New (and Chaotic) Frontier of Business," *Fast Company*, January 9, 2012.

Chapter 1

page 5 "Our cave ancestors were visually literate; their lives depended on how well . . ." Harry G. Tuttle, "Better Learning and Expressing of Learning Through Visual Literacy," September 7, 2006; retrieved September 15, 2007, from School of Education, Syracuse University, eduwithtech.wordpress.com.

page 11 "Young children think and cognitively process in pictures . . ." P. E. Klass, R.N., "The Developing Brain and Early Learning," *Archives of Disease in Childhood*, November 2003; retrieved August 24, 2012, from adc.bmj.com /content/88/8/651.1full.

page 12 "they connect these images to language and to culture" P. Liebermann, "On the Nature of Evolution of the Neural Bases of Human Language," *Yearbook of Physical Anthropology*, 2002, pp. 36–62.

page 12 "Today our students are visually literate within their world of 'electronic images' such as TV, videogames . . . ." Tuttle, "Better Learning."

page 13 "learning styles—visual, kinesthetic, and auditory . . ." T. F. Hawk and A. J. Shab, "Using Learning Styles Instruments to Enhance Student Learning," *Decision Sciences Journal of Innovative Education*, 2007, pp. 1540–4609.

page 13 "educational researchers suggest that approximately 83% . . ." U.S. Department of Labor, *Construction Safety and Health Outreach Program* (O. O. Education, Producer), May 1, 1996; retrieved September 15, 2012, from Occupational Safety & Health Administration, http://www.osha.gov/doc /outreachtraining/htmlfiles/traintec.html.

page 14 "In *The Decision Book* by Mikael Krogerus . . ." Mikael Krogerus, Roman Tschäppeler, Philip Earnhart, and Jenny Piening, *The Decision Book* (New York: Norton, 2011).

page 15 Images from ibid., pp. 91, 116–117.

page 19 "Root cause analysis . . ." M. L. Emiliani, "Origins of Lean Management in America: The Role of Connecticut in Business," *Journal of Management History* 12(2), 2006, pp. 167–184.

page 20 "the authors . . . interview Curtis Carlson, CEO of SRI International." Thomas L. Friedman and Michael Mandlebaum, *That Used to Be Us* (New York: Picador/Farrar, Straus & Giroux, 2012), pp. 96–98.

page 21 "Second, research from the field of Appreciative Inquiry . . ." Weatherhead School of Management, Case Western Reserve University, *Appreciative Inquiry Commons*, September 26, 2000; retrieved November 15, 2011, from www.appreciativeinquiry.case.edu.

pages 21–22 "Our mood, attitude, and willingness sour as we focus . . ." C. Wallis, "The New Science of Happiness," *Time*, January 17, 2005; retrieved October 23, 2012, from www.authentichappiness.sas.upenn.edu/images/TimeMagazine /Time-Happiness.pdf.

page 22 "reptilian brain" D. Baker, *What Happy People Know: How the New Science of Happiness Can Change Your Life for the Better* (New York: St. Martin's Griffin, 2004).

page 27 "In order for imagination to lead implementation, we need to deprive . . ." Annette Moser-Wellman, *The Five Faces of Genius* (New York: Penguin Books, 2011), pp. 66–69.

page 29 "An organization that's facing a real threat or eyeing a new opportunity . . ." John P. Kotter, "Accelerate!," *Harvard Business Review*, November 4, 2012, p. 1.

page 31 "We wonder why overall productivity is down, and why 71 percent of the American workforce . . ." N. Blacksmith and J. Harten, "Majority of Americans Not Engaged in Their Jobs," Gallup Wellbeing, October 28, 2011; retrieved

September 28, 2012. from http://www.gallup.com/poll/150383/majority
-american-workers-not-engaged-jobs.aspx.

page 32 "One of the biggest issues in almost . . ." Sabina Spencer, author's interview
on October 7, 2012.

page 32 "Twenty-first century businesses demand much more from their
leaders. . . ." Will McInnes, "Dear Business-as-Usual, It's Time for a Revolution," *BA Business Life*, October 14, 2012.

page 33 "The power of strategic illustration is that it encourages dialogue . . ."
Sabina Spencer, author's interview, October 30, 2012.

Chapter 3

page 54 "one of the 'founders' of the concept Group Graphics™ with Geoff Ball . . ."
David Sibbet, "A Graphic Facilitation Retrospective." Adapted from a presentation at the International Association of Facilitators, The Art and Mastery
of Facilitation—Navigating the Future, IAF Conference, May 16-20, 2001.

page 61 "Graphic facilitation supports the resolution of conflicts by going be-
yond a solely verbal . . ." Geoff Ball, "Graphic Facilitation Focuses a Group's
Thoughts," *Consensus*, April 18, 1998, p. 2; retrieved May 12, 2007, from
Mediate.com, http://www.mediate.com/articles/ball.cfm.

page 61 "Visual Literacy refers to a group of vision-competencies a human
being . . ." M. Avgerinou and J. Ericsson, "A Review of the Concept of Visual
Literacy," *British Journal of Education Technology* 25(4), 1997, pp. 280–291.

page 62 "that doodlers actually remember more than nondoodlers when asked
to retain tediously . . ." Jackie Andrade, "What Does Doodling Do?," *Applied
Cognitive Psychology Issues* 24, 2010, pp. 100–101.

page 62 "doodling forces your brain to expend just enough energy to stop it from
daydreaming . . ." Ibid., p. 106.

page 63 Information on left brain and right brain: B. Mauk, "Brain Scientists Identify Close Links Between the Arts, Learning," *Arts Education in the News*, May
14, 2009; retrieved April 22, 2011, from the Dana Foundation, https://www
.dana.org/news/features/detail.aspx?id=21822; E. Jensen, *Arts with the Brain in
Mind* (Washington, DC: Association for Supervision and Curriculum Development, 2011); L. Bowie, "Arts Appear to Play a Role in Brain Development,"
Baltimore Sun, May 18, 2009; H. Gardner, *Art, Mind and Brain: A Cognitive
Approach* (New York: Basic Books, 1984); S. Lipoff, "Right Brain or Left Brain:
Creativity," *So Says Sarah* (blog), September 18, 2011; retrieved July 14, 2012,
from http://sarahlipoff.com/2011/09/18/right-brainleft-brain-creativity/;

and American Psychological Association, "Brain's Left and Right Sides Working Together in Mathematically Gifted Youth," *Science Daily*, April 12, 2004; retrieved July 10, 2012, from http://www.sciencedaily.com/releases /2004/04/040412012459.htm.

page 64 "Visual imagery is another example [of how the left and the right brain work together simultaneously] . . ." Miriam Vered, "Left and Right Brain Working Together," *Brain Skills*; retrieved October 30, 2012, from www.brainskills .co.uk/leftandrightbrainworkingtogether.html.

page 65 "The prefrontal cortex . . . 'is involved in thinking about the future' . . ." Y. Yang and A. Raine, "Prefrontal structural and functional brain imaging findings in antisocial, violent, and psychopathic individuals: a meta-analysis." Retrieved June 4, 2012. *Psychiatry Res* 174 (2): 81. 2009.

page 65 "The limbic system (deep in the center . . .)" Farlex, "The Limbic Brain," *The Free Dictionary*, January 1, 2012; retrieved September 3, 2012, from http://www.thefreedictionary.com/limbic+brain.

page 65 "The content may provoke some type of emotion . . ." C. George Boeree, "The Emotional Nervous System"; retrieved November 1, 2012, from General Psychology, http://webspace.ship.edu/cgboer/limbicsystem.html.

Chapter 4

page 73 "That is why visualizing can improve performance." Norman Doidge, *The Brain That Changes Itself* (New York: Penguin Books, 2007), pp. 200–205.

page 74 "mental practice" Ibid., p. 204.

page 77 "Visuals are a great tool to support communication . . ." Sabine Soeder, author's interview, October 1, 2012.

page 79 "Now is the time to let the team members have the freedom to use their imagination." Ulric Rudebeck, *Strategic Vision Work* (Stockholm, Sweden: UR Vision, 2008), p. 120.

page 86 "The hierarchical structures and organizational processes we have used . . ." John P. Kotter, "Accelerate!," *Harvard Business Review*, November 4, 2012, p. 4.

page 87 "Perception is a part of how humans biologically survive." R. L. Gregory, *Eye and Brain: The Psychology of Seeing* (Princeton, NJ: Princeton University Press, 1990).

page 87 "we can survive in almost any environment, conditions, or circum stances . . ." D. Hebb, "Science and the World of Imagination," *Canadian Psychology* 16, 1975, pp. 4–11.

page 87 "Part of the evolutionary strategy involving survival . . ." H. R. Pagels, *The Dream of Reason* (New York: Bantam Books, 1988).

page 88 "As people are added to the mix, along with their various cultures, different languages . . ." J. Deregowski, "Real Space and Represented Space: Cross Cultural Perspectives," *Behavioral and Brain Sciences* 12, 1989, p. 57.

page 93 "John Chambers, the longstanding CEO of Cisco, reflected on this change in business . . ." A. Bryant, "In a Near-Death Event, a Corporate Rite of Passage," *New York Times*, August 1, 2009.

page 94 "In *That Used to Be Us*, Friedman and Mandlebaum . . ." Thomas L. Friedman and Michael Mandlebaum, *That Used to Be Us* (New York: Picador/Farrar, Straus & Giroux, 2012), p. 93.

page 95 "Stories are more powerful . . ." M. Koerth-Baker, "The Mind of a Flip-Flopper," *New York Times Magazine*, August 19, 2012, p. 14.

page 99 "They loved it! And they were so . . ." Martha Lanaghen, author's interview, October 4, 2012.

page 103 "We believe that intrinsic motivation must be present . . ." James M. Kouzes and Barry Z. Posner, *The Leadership Challenge* (San Francisco: Jossey-Bass, 1995), p. 40.

pages 103–104 "It's like it almost happened in a flash. . . ." Lois Todd, author's interview, July 12, 2012.

page 107 "We had one day to get 35 people . . ." Elizabeth Groginsky, author's interview, October 2, 2012.

page 109 "We have always been a hard organization . . ." Lisa Barwell, author's interview, September 25, 2012.

page 110 "Usually . . . fear is rooted in the need for the change . . ." John Hunt, *The Art of the Idea* (Brooklyn, NY: Powerhouse Books, 2009), p. 128.

page 112 "Our strategy map has built a whole new language . . ." Lisa Bardwell, author's interview, September 25, 2012.

page 117 "The map gives me a kind of emotional confidence. . . ." Ibid.

page 117 "Before every engagement with a client . . ." Carlos Mota, author's interview, October 29, 2012.

page 118 "Much of our sense of self-worth comes from our ability to be generative . . ." Sabina Spencer, *The Heart of Leadership* (London: Ebury Press, 2001), p. 84.

page 118 "DuPont has products that are derived from inferior-quality Corian and Tyvek. . . ." Conjecture Corporation, "What Are Tyvek Wristbands?," *wiseGEEK*; retrieved December 5, 2011, from www.wisegeek.com/what-are-tyvek-wristbands.htm.

page 118 "Post-its" Massachusetts Institute of Technology, School of Engineering, "Inventor of the Week: Art Fry and Spencer Silver," September 23, 2007;

retrieved December 19, 2011, from Lemelson-MIT Archives, http://web.mit
.edu/invent/iow/frysilver.html.

pages 118–119 "People within these companies spent time creating a product
from a mistake." H. Petroski, *The Evolution of Useful Things* (New York: Alfred A. Knopf, 1992).

page 120 "In the 2012 Olympics, Ryan Lochte . . ." "My Sportsman: Ryan Lochte,"
Sports Illustrated, August 17, 2012; retrieved October 12, 2012, from www
.sportsillustrated.cnn.com/2011/magazine/sportsman/11/12/anderson
-lochte/index.html.

page 120 "It worked. In the *Art of Possibility*, conductor . . ." R. S. Zander and B.
Zander, *The Art of Possibility* (New York: Penguin Books, 2000), pp. 9–23.

Chapter 5

page 126 "It's not so much about the quality of the drawing. . . ." Todd Barker, author's interview, November 2, 2012.

Page 127 "Aligning people to a shared set of aspirations . . ." Peter Senge, et al., *The
Dance of Change* (New York: Doubleday 1999), p. 409.

page 128 "physical construction of systems and relationships in an . . ." "Alignment," Wikipedia, September 30, 2012; retrieved October 23, 2012, from
en.wikipedia.org/wiki/alignment.

page 129 "the ancient alchemists, the triangle represented . . ." J. Emick, "A Visual
Glossary: Alchemical Fire," *Symboldictionary*, January 10, 2009; retrieved
July 22, 2012, from http://symboldictionary.net/?p=2504.

page 132 "Visual language helps people build on each other's ideas. . . ." Juanita
Brown, author's interview, October 31, 2012.

page 134 "8 percent of the land is privately owned, 25 percent is tribal, and 67 percent is public land. . . ." Utah Governor's Office of Planning and Budget, "San
Juan County Profile," December 2003, www.planning.utah.gov.

page 137 "Community buy-in is the only way this project will succeed. . . ." Janet
Ross, author's interview, June 2007.

page 138 "Acceleration can be defined as 'a measure of how fast velocity changes."
"Acceleration," Wikipedia, September 15, 2012; retrieved September 23,
2012, from www.en.wikipedia.org/wiki/accelerator.

page 139 "the phenomenon that a variable moves toward its desired value . . ." "Accelerator Effect," Wikipedia, January 27, 2012; retrieved September 15, 2012,
from www.en.wikipedia.org/wiki/accelerator_effect.

page 140 "The excitement of the possibility of expressing . . ." Carlos Mota, author's
interview, November 2, 2012.

page 141 "I have seen many instances . . ." Jeraldene Lovell-Cole, author's interview, October 20, 2012.

page 142 "operate in concert" John P. Kotter, "Accelerate!," *Harvard Business Review*, November 4, 2012, p. 4.

page 142 "There is an operating system (or 'management-driven hierarchy') . . ." Ibid., p. 6.

page 142 "guiding coalition" Ibid.

page 142 "strategy network" Ibid., pp. 1–8.

page 144 "The inevitable failures of single operating systems hurt us now. They are going to . . ." Ibid., p. 8.

Chapter 6

page 150 "I draw in my home office to . . ." Todd Barker, author's interview, November 2, 2012.

page 151 "Attention is directed from your person to your subject." Mikael Krogerus, Roman Tschäppeler, Philip Earnhart, and Jenny Piening, *The Decision Book* (New York: Norton, 2011), p. 156.

page 152 "Drawing together brings things down to the 'human scale . . ." Juanita Brown, author's interview, October 31, 2012.

pages 153–158 Visual coaching guides: E. Auzan, C. Chopyak, et al., Germany: Neuland, 2011), http://www.neuland.com/US/details.htm?$product=7g 034msxtus.

page 158 "*The Balanced Scorecard*" Robert S. Kaplan, David P. Norton, *The Balanced Scorecard: Translating Strategy into Action* (Boston: Harvard Business Review Press, 1996).

page 160 "These [activity] maps combine time, content, and the physical condition or space . . ." Ulric Rudebeck, author's interview, October 13, 2012.

page 166 "Influence and concern map." Stephen R. Covey, *7 Habits of Highly Effective People* (New York: Free Press, 1989).

page 168 "Force field analysis." M. Connelly, "Force Field Analysis—Kurt Lewin"; retrieved September 2011 from http://www.change-management-coach .com/force-field-analysis.html; and J. Neal, "Field Theory—Kurt Lewin"; retrieved October 14, 2011 from http://www.wilderdom.com/theory/Field Theory.html.

page 170 "History is like a container. . . . It is a well to draw from . . ." Ulric Rudebeck, *Strategic Vision Work* (Stockholm, Sweden: UR Vision, 2008), p. 63.

page 172 "All the pictures capture, keep together, and transfer the ideas, experiences . . ." Ibid., p. 32.

page 173 "This happens when the people . . ." Lois Todd, author's interview, September 14, 2012.

page 178 "You can only draw stick-men?" Krogerus, et al., *The Decision Book*, p. 156.

page 182 "When you are moving toward the change . . ." Elizabeth Groginsky, author's interview, October 2, 2012.

page 183 "We think with the objects we love; we love the objects we think with." Sherry Turkle, *Evocative Objects: Things We Think With* (Cambridge, MA: Massachusetts Institute of Technology, 2007), p. 19.

page 183 "Objects are able to catalyze self-creation." Ibid., p. 28.

American Psychological Association. "Brain's Left and Right Sides Working Together in Mathematically Gifted Youth." *Science Daily*, April 12, 2004. Retrieved July 10, 2012, from http://www.sciencedaily.com/releases/2004/04/040412012459.htm.

Andrade, Jackie. "What Does Doodling Do?" *Applied Cognitive Psychology Issues* 24, 2010, pp. 100–106.

Auzan, E., Chopyak, C., et al. *Visual Coaching Guides*. Germany: Neuland, 2011, http://www.neuland.com/US/details.htm?$product=7g034msxtus.

Avgerinou, M., and J. Ericsson. "A Review of the Concept of Visual Literacy." *British Journal of Education Technology* 25(4), 1997, pp. 280–291.

Baker, D. *What Happy People Know: How the New Science of Happiness Can Change Your Life for the Better*. New York: St. Martin's Griffin, 2004.

Ball, Geoff. "Graphic Facilitation Focuses a Group's Thoughts." *Consensus*, April 18, 1998. Retrieved May 12, 2007, from Mediate.com: http://www.mediate.com/articles/ball.cfm.

Blacksmith, N., and J. Harten. "Majority of Americans Not Engaged in Their Jobs." Gallup Wellbeing, October 28, 2011. Retrieved September 28, 2012, from http://www.gallup.com/poll/150383/majority-american-workers-not-engaged-jobs.aspx.

Boeree, C. George. "The Emotional Nervous System." Retrieved November 1, 2012, from General Psychology, http://webspace.ship.edu/cgboer/limbicsystem.html.

Bowie, L. "Arts Appear to Play a Role in Brain Development." *Baltimore Sun*, May 18, 2009.

Brown, J., and D. Isaacs. *The World Cafe Book: Shaping Our Futures Through Conversations That Matter*. San Francisco: Berrett-Koehler, 2005.

Bryant, A. "In a Near-Death Event, a Corporate Rite of Passage." *New York Times*, August 1, 2009.

Case Western Reserve University, Weatherhead School of Management. *Appreciative Inquiry Commons*, September 26, 2000. Retrieved November 15, 2011, from www.appreciativeinquiry.case.edu.

Conjecture Corporation. "What Are Tyvek Wristbands?" *wiseGEEK*. Retrieved December 5, 2011, from www.wisegeek.com/what-are-tyvek-wristbands.htm.

Connelly, M. "Force Field Analysis—Kurt Lewin." Retrieved in September 2011 from http://www.change-management-coach.com/force-field-analysis.html.

Covey, S. R. *7 Habits of Highly Effective People*. New York: Free Press, 1989.

Deregowski, J. "Real Space and Represented Space: Cross Cultural Perspectives." *Behavioral and Brain Sciences* 12, 1989, p. 57.

Doidge, Norman. *The Brain That Changes Itself*. New York: Penguin Books, 2007.

DuPont. *History & Facts*, January 5, 2012. Retrieved November 20, 2012, from DuPont Surfaces, http://www2.dupont.com/Surfaces/en_US/whats_new/news_and_media/history_facts/.

Emick, J. "A Visual Glossary: Alchemical Fire." *Symboldictionary*, January 10, 2009. Retrieved July 22, 2012, from http://symboldictionary.net/?p=2504.

Emiliani, M. L. "Origins of Lean Management in America: The Role of Connecticut in Business." *Journal of Management History* 12(2), 2006, pp. 167–184.

Farlex. "The Limbic Brain." *The Free Dictionary*, January 1, 2012. Retrieved September 3, 2012, from http://www.thefreedictionary.com/limbic+brain.

Friedman, Thomas L., and Michael Mandlebaum. *That Used to Be Us*. New York: Picador/Farrar, Straus & Giroux, 2012.

Gardner, H. *Art, Mind and Brain: A Cognitive Approach*. New York: Basic Books, 1984.

Gregory, R. L. *Eye and Brain: The Psychology of Seeing*. Princeton, NJ: Princeton University Press, 1990.

Hawk, T. F., and A. J. Shab. "Using Learning Styles Instruments to Enhance Student Learning." *Decision Sciences Journal of Innovative Education*, 2007, pp. 1540–4609.

Hebb, D. "Science and the World of Imagination." *Canadian Psychology* 16, 1975, pp. 4–11.

Hunt, John. *The Art of the Idea*. Brooklyn, NY: Powerhouse Books, 2009.

Jensen, E. *Arts with the Brain in Mind*. Washington, DC: Association for Supervision and Curriculum Development, 2011.

Kaplan, R. S. and D. P. Norton. *The Balanced Scorecard: Translating Strategy into Action* Boston, MA: Harvard Business Review Press, 1996.

Kazlev, M. A. "The Triune Brain." KHEPER, October 19, 2003. Retrieved October 2, 2012, from http://www.kheper.net/topics/intelligence/MacLean.htm.

Koerth-Baker, M. "The Mind of a Flip-Flopper." *New York Times Magazine*, August 19, 2012, p. 14.

Kotter, John P. "Accelerate!" *Harvard Business Review*, November 4, 2012, pp. 1–8.

Kouzes, James M., and Barry Z. Posner. *The Leadership Challenge*. San Francisco: Jossey-Bass, 1995.

Klass, P. E. "The Developing Brain and Early Learning." *Archives of Disease in Childhood*. Retrieved August 24, 2012, from adc.bmj.com/content/88/8/651.1full.

Krogerus, Mikael, Roman Tschäppeler, Philip Earnhart, and Jenny Piening. *The Decision Book*. New York: Norton, 2011.

Liebermann, P. "On the Nature of Evolution of the Neural Bases of Human Language." *Yearbook of Physical Anthropology*, 2002, pp. 36–62.

Lipoff, S. "Right Brain or Left Brain: Creativity." *So Says Sarah* (blog), September 18, 2011. Retrieved July 14, 2012, from http://sarahlipoff.com/2011/09/18/right-brainleft-brain-creativity//.

Margulies, N., and C. Valenza. *Visual Thinking: Tools for Mapping Your Ideas*. Williston, VT: Crown House Publishing, 2005.

Massachusetts Institute of Technology, School of Engineering. "Inventor of the Week: Art Fry and Spencer Silver," September 23, 2007. Retrieved December 19, 2011, from Lemelson-MIT Archives, http://web.mit.edu/invent/iow/frysilver.html.

Mauk, B. "Brain Scientists Identify Close Links Between the Arts, Learning." *Arts Education in the News*, May 14, 2009. Retrieved April 22, 2011, from the Dana Foundation, https://www.dana.org/news/features/detail.aspx?id=21822.

McInnes, W. "Dear Business-as-Usual, It's Time for a Revolution." *BA Business Life*, October 14, 2012.

Moser-Wellman, Annette. *The Five Faces of Genius*. New York: Penguin Books, 2011.

Neal, J. "Field Theory—Kurt Lewin," April 20, 2004. Retrieved October 14, 2011 from http://www.wilderdom.com/theory/FieldTheory.html.

Pagels, H. R. *The Dream of Reason*. New York: Bantam Books, 1988.

Petroski, H. *The Evolution of Useful Things*. New York: Alfred A. Knopf, 1992.

Raine, Y. A. "Prefrontal structural and functional brain imaging findings in antisocial, violent, and psychopathic individuals: a meta-analysis." Retrieved June 4, 2012. *Psychiatry Res* 174 (2), 2009, pp. 81–88.

Roam, D. *Back of the Napkin*. New York: Penguin Books, 2008.

Rudebeck, Ulric. *Strategic Vision Work*. Stockholm: UR Vision, 2008.

Safian, R. "This Is Generation Flux: Meet the Pioneers of the New (and Chaotic) Frontier of Business." *Fast Company*, January 9, 2012.

Sagan, C. *The Dragons of Eden*. New York: Random House, 1977.

Senge, Peter, et. al. *The Dance of Change*. New York: Doubleday, 1999.

Sibbet, D. "A Graphic Facilitation Retrospective." Adapted from a presentation at the International Association of Facilitators Conference, *The Art and Mastery of Facilitation: Navigating the Future,* May 16–20, 2001.

Spencer, Sabina. *The Heart of Leadership*. London: Ebury Press, 2001.

Sports Illustrated. "My Sportsman: Ryan Lochte," August 17, 2012. Retrieved October 12, 2012, from www.sportsillustrated.cnn.com/2011/magazine /sportsman/11/12/anderson-lochte/index.html.

Turkle, Sherry. *Evocative Objects: Things We Think With*. Cambridge, MA: Massachusetts Institute of Technology, 2007.

Tuttle, Harry G. "Better Learning and Expressions of Learning through Visual Literacy," September 7, 2006. Retrieved September 15, 2007, from School of Education, Syracuse University, eduwithtech.wordpress.com.

U.S. Department of Labor. *Construction Safety and Health Outreach Program* (O. O. Education, Producer), May 1, 1996. Retrieved September 15, 2012, from Occupational Safety & Health Administration, http://www.osha.gov/doc /outreachtraining/htmlfiles/traintec.html.

Vered, Miriam. "Left and Right Brain Working Together." *Brain Skills*, October 1, 2012. Retrieved October 30, 2012, from www.brainskills.co.uk/leftandright brainworkingtogether.html.

Wallis, C. "The New Science of Happiness." *Time*, January 17, 2005. Retrieved October 23, 2012, from www.authentichappiness.sas.upenn.edu/images /TimeMagazine/Time-Happiness.pdf.

Whitney, D. L., and D. Cooperrider. *Appreciative Inquiry*. San Francisco: Berrett-Koehler Communications Inc., 1999.

Wikipedia. "Accelerator Effect," January 27, 2012. Retrieved September 15, 2012, from www.en.wikipedia.org/wiki/accelerator_effect.

———"Alignment," September 30, 2012. Retrieved October 23, 2012, from en.wikipedia.org/wiki/alignment.

Zander, R. S., and B. Zander. *The Art of Possibility*. New York: Penguin Books, 2000.

Zemke, R. A., and S. Zemke. "30 Things We Know for Sure About Adult Learning." *Honolulu University Teaching Tips*, March 9, 1984. Retrieved January 5, 2008, from http://www2.honolulu.hawaii.edu/facdev/guidebk/teachtip /m-files/m-adult3.htm.

ACKNOWLEDGMENTS

This book is a miracle in so many ways. It is the culmination of long conversations, experimentation, and challenging the status quo with so many others.

My deepest thanks and gratitude go first and foremost to my writing coach, Clydette de Groot, who coached, questioned, critiqued, and laughed with me throughout this amazing process. To my guardian angel, Sabina Spencer, who pushed me through the door to speak with McGraw-Hill and showed unwavering confidence and encouragement throughout the process. And, thank you, Jeraldene, for reminding me that I have a calling.

The formation of these ideas originated in conversations at a kitchen table in Dresden, Germany (thank you, Sabine and Ulrich), in museums around Europe and the United States (thank you, Ulric), and in cafés in Geneva (thank you, Elizabeth). Thanks to all the "alchemists" who have taken classes and challenged many of the assumptions that are featured and discussed in this book. Your tenacity, dedication, and creativity are what keep me inspired and continuing to improve my craft.

Thanks to all of my clients, colleagues, and friends. You made this book and its content possible. Without the ability to share, capture, guide, provoke, question, and support your work, the insights and ideas shared here would not have materialized.

Listening is an important part of this work, and my debt of gratitude goes to David Isaacs, a master of deep listening and reflection; to Carlos Mota, one of the finest question crafters I have had the privilege of working with; and to Juanita Brown for pushing my thinking and doing into new spaces and new places.

Thanks to Emily Vercoe for her tireless research, to Alece Birnbach for the cover design and a final boost of confidence, and to Lois Todd for her boundless energy for "possibilities." I am indebted to Alchemy for the belief and support that everyone on the team has provided me during the creation of this book.

Donya Dickerson, senior editor at McGraw-Hill Education, is a remarkable, smart, and savvy businesswoman who took a risk on me to tell the business story of pictures, strategy, and execution. Donya made the writing process easy, fun, and exciting with high trust and confidence in the concept and the writer. You are a gem and a wonderful person.

In the same way that "business" can become "family," my family has been drawn into my business. Thanks to Joellen (sister 1), who gave me permission to be crazy and just write. To my brother, for his disbelief and admiration. To Jill (sister 2), for her affirmation that I was supposed to write this book. To my mother, Angie, the editor (without her, I would still be dealing with tenses and typos), and to my father, Joe, for his last-minute "weighing in."

My husband, John Herge, deserves the last, super "high five" as one of the most patient, steadfast, smart, provocative, and interesting people I know. The ideas shared here come from hours of conversations, drawing, and support we have done together. It doesn't get any better than you!

INDEX

About the Author

 **Christine Chopyak** is a skilled consultant and strategist who uses a variety of methodologies, best practices, graphics, and deep listening to elicit ideas, solutions, and innovation from people and their organizations. Her approach results in a dynamic environment in which high energy, best practices, and system practicalities create opportunities that both clients and stakeholders are enthusiastic about deploying.

Given her more than 20 years of business planning, consulting, public participation, and stakeholder engagement experience and her systems background, Chris's clients include multinational Fortune 500 companies, government agencies, municipalities, county governments, trade associations, and school systems. She has designed processes for and with multiple industries, including finance, technology, energy and utilities, pharmaceuticals, consumer products, large consulting businesses, petrochemicals, agriculture, publishing, and education, as well as aerospace and hotels. With a specialty in large-group facilitation (more than 150) and cultural integration, Chris enjoys the challenge of dealing with both large systems and small teams in diverse, multicultural, and international settings.

One key differentiator for Chris is the incorporation of strategic illustration and animation to mobilize those she works with. While including art and pictures in her projects, she adeptly weaves expert design principles, stories and storytelling, play, empathy, and symphony as a way to focus on what matters most to the client in the context of the immediate business needs.

Prior to her leadership role at Alchemy, Chris served as the vice president for development at Earth Force and executive director of Keystone Science School, a division of the Keystone Center located in Keystone, Colorado. She has served as a keynote speaker and guest faculty member at several business schools across the United States. She serves on the board of a variety of nonprofit organizations. Chris has an MBA from the Executive and Professional Education program at the Daniels College of Business, University of Denver, and is a graduate of the *50 for Colorado* executive education program at the LEEDS Business School at the University of Colorado at Boulder. Visit www.link2alchemy.com to learn more about her, her company, and their work.